CANADIAN KITCHEN GARDEN

Easy, Fresh & Organic

Laura Peters
Alison Beck

PARTNERS
PUBLISHING

Co-published by Partners Publishing and Lone Pine Media Productions (B.C.) Ltd.

Distributed by: Canada Book Distributors - Booklogic
11414-119 Street
Edmonton, AB   T5G 2X6   Canada
Tel: 1-800-661-9017

Canadian Cataloguing in Publication Data
Peters, Laura, 1968–, author
The Canadian kitchen garden / Laura Peters and Alison Beck.
Includes index.
ISBN 978-1-77213-006-5 (paperback)
1. Kitchen gardens—Canada. 2. Vegetable gardening—Canada. I. Beck, Alison, 1971–, author II. Title.
SB323.C3P47 2017   635.0971   C2016-907250-9

Project Editor: Sheila Cooke
Production Manager: Leslie Hung
Layout and Production: Tamara Hartson, Gregory Brown
Cover Design: Gregory Brown

Photography: All photos are by Laura Peters and Nanette Samol except: All-America Selections 171a; Frank De Meyer 77a; Elliot Engley 37a&b; Jen Fafard 146; Andrzej Fryda 114; Tamara Hartson 16b, 25a&b, 26b, 29a, 47b, 108, 147a, 159a&b, 161b, 198, 199b, 208, 207a,b&c, 213b, 214, 216, 217b, 218, 219a, 227b, 229b; Hemera 131b (Krzysztof Slusarczyk); iStock 5, 11a (nevarpp), 11b (mitrs3), 15b (Holcy), 20a (Grahamphoto23), 21 (demaerre), 32a (Mypurgatoryyears), 32b (scottbeard), 33 (John Braid), 35a (CobraCZ), 36 (Wojtek Skora), 49 (kazakovmaksim), 68 (Dragoncello), 69a (tanjichica7), 69b (jojoo64), 71a (juliedeshales), 84 (Holcy), 86 (Vaivirga), 102&103a (y-studio), 116 (Neonci), 124 (Nicholas77), 125a (MaximShebeko), 125b (mitrs3), 130 (cbenjasuwan), 131a (id-art), 131c (aetb), 136 (StudioBarcelona), 137b (yanjf), 144 (EvgeniySmolskiy), 145a (Teamjackson), 145b (13-smile), 154 (Murphy_Shewchuk), 155a (HaiGala), 157a (Marina Lohrbach), 157b (doidam10), 165a (Pongmanat018), 169b (scull2), 171b (-Invst-), 173a (Zerbor), 175b (Oliver Hoffmann), 176 (Gitagraph), 178 (DaneeShe), 179a (natasarepovz), 179b (DanielRJones), 181b (AGEphotography), 188 (CobraCZ), 192 (LianeM), 193a, 195 (EdwardSamuelCornwall), 193b (Marnel Tomic), 210, 211b (DaisyLiang), 220 (areeya_ann); Liz Klose 7a, 29b, 202, 203b; Olga Langerova 134; L. Lauzuma 135a; Janet Loughrey 4; Tim Matheson 14b, 19a&b, 20b, 22a, 39a,b&c, 40b, 42a,b&c, 48a, 151b, 155b, 158, 160, 161a, 162, 163a, 197a, 212, 213a, 215a, 221a, 223b, 225b, 226; Steve Nikkila 150; Kim O'Leary 222; Allison Penko 141a; photos.com 48c, 169a; Robert Richie 47a, 163b, 182, 228, 229a; Paul Swanson 50, 51b, 59a, 60, 63a, 65b, 73a&b, 83a, 95b, 99b, 101a, 109b, 113a, 117a, 118, 119a, 132, 204; Yen-Hung Wang 89a; Sandy Weatherall 9b, 10a, 17a, 28b, 31b, 44b, 52, 53a, 57a, 59b, 62a&b, 79a, 90, 93b, 95a, 96, 106b, 107b, 109a, 110a, 111b, 123a, 142, 153c, 156, 167a, 187a, 197b; Don Williamson 143a&b, 225a; Carol Woo 48b; Tim Wood 14a.

Maps (pp. 12, 13): adapted from Natural Resources Canada.

We acknowledge the financial support of the Government of Canada.

Funded by the Government of Canada
Financé par le gouvernement du Canada | Canada

PC: 28

Table of Contents

Introduction

Edible gardens have been part of human culture for thousands of years. Growing plants that provide food and learning to store that food for times of scarcity were advancements that allowed humans to develop civilizations.

Today, most of our food comes from the grocery store. When we buy food from the grocery store, we give little thought to where it came from, how far it had to travel and how much it cost to transport it, first to the store and then to the table. We don't think about how it was grown or who grew it. Growing our own food plants in our very own kitchen gardens develops a greater appreciation for the food, our gardens and the ability to provide for ourselves and our families.

There are many more good reasons to grow your own food. You can save money on your grocery bill; it's environmentally friendly because fewer resources are used growing and getting the food to your table; it saves wildlife habitat by reducing the need to expand cultivated land; you have chance to seek out varieties and specialty items; and an often-overlooked reason to grow edible plants is that they are attractive and often unique in appearance.

Many gardeners are put off by the thought of digging up a rectangle and having an uninspiring display of rows in their carefully landscaped backyard. Other gardeners simply don't have the space for a large in-ground vegetable plot. Kitchen gardening can be done on any scale, in any space. You can add plenty of edible plants to the landscape you already have; single plants and small groups can make attractive features. Also, many edibles make great container plants, perfect for the balcony or kitchen windowsill.

A kitchen garden can include much more than just leafy vegetables and certain herbs. A multitude of vegetables and herbs, as well as fruits, seeds and flowers will thrive in your garden, no matter where you live, how small your garden or what form it takes. Think about your favourite vegetables and fruits. You don't have to try to accommodate your food needs for an entire year, but you could supplement what

you buy by growing a few plants. You can start by adding vegetables to patio containers and borders, or even setting up a few small pots of herbs and microgreens on a sunny windowsill. Do you eat a lot of broccoli? Three to six plants can provide two people with a lot of meals because many selections produce additional smaller heads once the main one is cut. A container of tomatoes combined with flowering annuals on a sunny balcony or deck is both beautiful and functional. Four zucchini plants will leave you wondering what to do with all your extra zucchini.

As with any gardening, growing a kitchen garden should be fun. Edible plants can add unique colours and textures to your garden and your dinner plate. Experiment with a few each year, and you may find yourself looking for space to add even more.

Kitchen Garden Style

A kitchen garden is many things to many people. The French potager, or kitchen garden, is a garden that is both decorative and functional. It generally consists of a symmetrical arrangement of raised beds. Plants are often repeated in a location in the bed rather than having one bed of all the same plant. Vegetables are combined with herbs and fruiting shrubs as well as edible flowers. There is no need to segregate edible plants from ornamental ones.

In this book, a kitchen garden is any space devoted to growing food plants. Kitchen gardens come in many forms and include a wide variety of plants. The neat rows of a traditional vegetable garden were adopted from the farm garden, and the attention paid to plant and row spacing is designed to make large numbers of plants more easily accessible. If you have plenty of space and want loads of vegetables to store over winter, this style can work for you.

In intensive gardens, plantings are done in groups rather than rows, and may be formal or informal. An example of a more formal intensive garden is a square-metre garden. A square raised bed measuring 1 metre along each side is divided into 9 or even 16 smaller planting squares. Each square is planted with as much of a single crop as the space will allow. As soon as a crop has matured and is harvested, something new is planted to replace it as long as the growing season allows.

An informal intensive garden could resemble a cottage-style garden, with vegetables and herbs planted in groups and drifts throughout existing beds. Tucking groups of edibles into existing beds takes

A traditional vegetable garden works well given plenty of space.

Many edibles double as ornamentals (above & below).

advantage of in-ground growing space without devoting a large chunk of your precious backyard space to a traditional vegetable garden. As an added advantage, many edibles can be ornamental.

Ornamental Edibles

- Amaranth
- Asparagus
- Bean
- Cabbage
- Cherry
- Dill
- Fiddlehead Fern
- Flax
- Kale
- Leek
- Rose
- Swiss Chard

Raised beds are an ideal way to grow edibles, as long as the drainage is adequate (leave the bottom open without sealing it or closing it in). Gardening in raised beds means less work. Beds can be raised up to whatever height suits you. When you raise the level of the garden, there's little need to bend over or squat, and with the addition

of a shallow ledge on all sides, a gentle bend is all it takes to weed or harvest a metre-high garden. Also, the season can be extended somewhat by growing your vegetables in raised beds simply because they thaw out earlier than the ground itself. Granted it's not a huge difference, but sometimes every day counts in the growing season.

As your garden grows and develops and you need to add new plants, think about adding edibles. If you need a new shrub, perhaps you could include a raspberry or blueberry bush; asparagus, fiddlehead fern and rhubarb are hardy perennial choices; and the wealth of annual options is nearly limitless.

Kitchen Gardening with Limited Space

There are many options for gardeners with limited gardening space. With populations growing and city densities increasing, more and more people are learning about the possibilities of their small spaces and discovering just how productive they can be. You don't need a large backyard to grow edibles—you just need to get creative. Vegetables, fruits and herbs can grow in just about any space, whether in the ground or in some form of container.

Containers can be placed anywhere and take up little space, can be moved around and sometimes offer more control than gardening directly in the ground. Just

Raised beds make plants more accessible and can extend the gardening season.

favourite edibles. It is entirely possible to have a productive kitchen garden on the balcony of a south-facing condo. Almost anything can be grown in pots, resulting in a steady stream of vegetables and herbs to pick from early on in the season to last frost. However, be careful to leave enough room to walk through the maze of pots for watering, fertilizing and harvesting. Even if you decide to start with only one tomato plant on your patio, front porch or balcony, you will find yourself planning to grow more and more as the years go on.

Grow mint in containers to control its spread.

Plants for Containers
- Mint and other aggressive plants
- Peppers and other tender annuals
- Rosemary and other tender perennials
- Dwarf varieties of large plants

Try growing peppers on a south-facing balcony.

about anything can be used as a container, as long as there is adequate drainage and enough space for the plant that will be spending its life there. Use a good quality potting soil for containers, and add compost to the mix as a natural source of nutrients. Stay away from the potting soils with added synthetic fertilizers, moisture crystals and so on. Keep it simple. Do not use soil from the garden, as it can compact, making it tough for roots to thrive.

Apartment and condominium dwellers should not shy away from growing their

Trailing (above) and climbing (below) plants take advantage of vertical space.

If the only open space you have is vertical, then vertical gardening is the solution. Smaller, trailing and leafy plants can all be grown in containers that hang or attach to a wall or other vertical surface, such as a fence. I've even known people to grow small plants or fruiting vines in old eaves troughs that were attached to the wall.

They're ideal for successive sowings and they're out of the way, not to mention incredibly easy to get to and pick from. Trellises, pyramids, obelisks and other vertical supports are great for vegetables and fruits that can grow upward rather than outward, rendering your precious space more efficient and resulting in

Plants for Vertical Growing

- Bean
- Cape Gooseberry
- Cucumber
- Grape
- Hardy Kiwi
- Melon
- Nasturtium
- Pea
- Squash
- Strawberry
- Tomato
- Watermelon

Herbs (above) and microgreens (below) are good candidates for indoor growing.

higher yields and easier harvesting. For example, beans, peas and cucumbers are great for supports such as netting, trellises and chainlink fences. Hanging baskets and window boxes are also ideal vertical spaces. Tomatoes and strawberries are common plants for such containers, whether they're a cascading variety or an upright type. Vertical gardening is of particular benefit to tomatoes because if left to flop on the ground, the air circulation is diminished, resulting in rot and insect infestation. As long as the right elements are present, anything is possible.

Another way to expand your gardening space is inward. Many edible plants, herbs in particular but also several vegetables, will happily grow indoors on a sunny kitchen windowsill or in a sunroom with shelves dedicated to your kitchen garden. In fact, microgreens and sprouts, two of the most popular edibles for a kitchen garden, are best grown indoors. The biggest challenge to growing plants indoors is a lack of light; most edibles require at least five hours of direct sunlight. The bonus of indoor growing, of course, is year-round harvest. There's nothing quite like home-grown, fresh produce in the dead of a Canadian winter.

Plants for Indoor Growing

- Basil
- Bay Laurel
- Cilantro
- Lettuce
- Microgreens
- Mint
- Oregano
- Parsley
- Pepper (chili)
- Rosemary
- Sprouts
- Thyme

Types of Edible Plants

Edible plants come in all forms, but most of the plants included in this book are annuals, biennials, perennials or woody shrubs.

Annuals

True annuals germinate, mature, bloom, set seed and die in one growing season. The plants we treat as annuals may be annuals, biennials or tender perennials. We plant them in spring or summer and expect to enjoy them for just that year. Many biennials, if started early enough, will flower the year you plant them, and many plants that are perennial in warmer climates will grow and flower before they succumb to our cold winter temperatures.

Annuals are categorized based on how they tolerate cold weather: hardy, half-hardy or tender. Hardy annuals tolerate low temperatures and even frost. They can be planted in the garden early and may continue to flower long into fall or winter. Many hardy annuals are sown directly in the garden before the last frost date. Half-hardy annuals will be killed by a heavy frost. Generally started early from seed indoors, they can be planted out around the last frost date. Tender annuals have no frost tolerance and suffer if the temperature drops even to a few degrees above freezing. They are often started early indoors and are not planted in the garden until the last frost date has passed and the

Average annual frost-free days

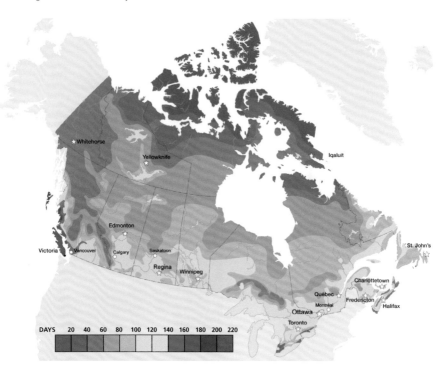

DAYS   20   40   60   80   100   120   140   160   180   200   220

ground has warmed up. Their advantage is that they often withstand hot summer temperatures.

Canadian last frost and first frost dates vary greatly. The map on page 12 shows average annual frost-free days. Protecting annuals from frost is simple—just cover them overnight with sheets, towels, burlap or even cardboard boxes. Don't use plastic because it doesn't retain heat or provide insulation.

Perennials

Perennials are plants that develop a persistent root and bloom once they are mature. This broad definition includes trees and shrubs, but more narrowly we mean herbaceous perennials that generally die back to the ground at the end of each growing season and start fresh with new shoots each spring. Some plants grouped with

perennials do not die back completely, and others remain green all winter. Subshrubs, such as thyme and sage, are plants that have woody bases but produce herbaceous or soft new growth that turns woody in its second season. Despite wide variation in winter garden conditions across Canada, some perennials will flourish and provide an almost limitless selection of colours, sizes and forms. This versatility, along with their beauty and permanence, lies at the root of their enduring popularity.

Hardiness zones are a guideline to follow when choosing perennial edible plants for your kitchen garden. The zones are based on the average climate conditions of each area and which plants will most likely survive there. Canada's hardiness map (page 13) is divided into nine major zones, and

Hardiness zones

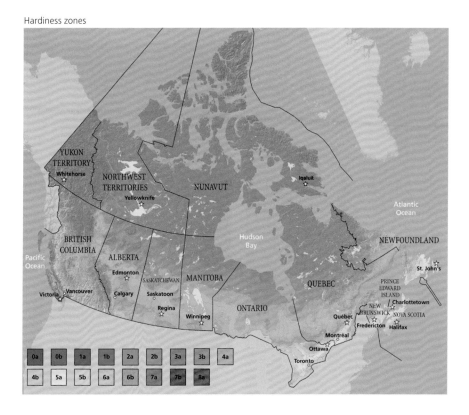

there are subzones and microclimates in every zone. Garden microclimates are influenced by such conditions as the nearness to buildings, how quickly the soil drains and whether it is in a low, cold hollow or on top of a windswept hill.

Nowadays, gardeners often grow tender perennials that successfully survive our cold winters even outside their optimal zones. It's exciting to experiment with microclimates. It is all a matter of not being discouraged when something fails from time to time.

Trees and Shrubs

Trees and shrubs are woody perennials that live for three or more years and maintain a permanent live structure above ground all year. A tree is generally defined as a tall woody plant that has a single trunk. A shrub is multi-stemmed and shorter. These definitions are not absolute—some tall trees are multi-stemmed, some short shrubs have single trunks, and one species may grow as a tree in favourable conditions and as a shrub in harsher sites.

Woody plants are characterized by leaf type: deciduous or evergreen, needled or broad-leaved. Deciduous plants lose all their leaves each fall. Evergreen trees and shrubs do not lose their leaves and can also be needled or broad-leaved. Semi-evergreen plants are normally evergreen, but in cold climates they lose some or all of their leaves.

Other Edible Plants

Fruiting vines can be annual or perennial, herbaceous or woody. Vegetables are the result of plants that produce edible seeds, roots, stems, leaves, bulbs, tubers or non-sweet fruits. Aquatic or water plants grow in water or wet soil. Bulbs have a bulb-like base that is either at soil level or under the soil. Other types of edibles include tropical plants that are grown as houseplants in colder climates.

Woody perennials like elderberries (below) and grapes (right) provide harvests year after year.

The Basics

Kale grows best in full sun.

Finding the right edibles for your kitchen garden requires experimentation and creativity, but also good planning and preparation. Before you start planting, consider the growing conditions in your garden; these conditions will influence not only the types of plants you select, but also the location in which you plant them. Plants will be healthier and less susceptible to problems if grown in optimum conditions.

Your plant selection should be influenced by the levels of light, the type of soil, and the amount of exposure in your garden. It is difficult to significantly modify most of your garden's existing conditions; an easier approach is to match the plants to the garden. Understanding your garden's growing conditions will help prevent costly mistakes—plan ahead rather than correct later.

Light

There are four basic categories of light in a garden: full sun, partial shade, light shade and full shade. Full sun locations, e.g., along a south-facing wall, receive direct sunlight all or most of the day. Partial shade or partial sun locations, e.g., along an east- or west-facing wall, receive direct sunlight for part of the day (four to six hours) and shade for the rest. Light shade locations receive shade for most or all of the day, but some sunlight does filter through to ground level; e.g., under a small-leaved tree such as a birch. Full shade locations, e.g., the north side of a house, receive little or no direct sunlight.

Buildings, trees, fences and the position of the sun at different times of the day and year affect available light. Also, the intensity of the sun varies; heat can become trapped and magnified between city buildings, baking all but the most heat-tolerant of plants. Knowing what light is available in your garden, as well as its intensity, will help you determine where to place each plant.

Fiddlehead ferns will thrive in shade.

Potato plants are useful for breaking up soil.

Soil

Plants and the soil they grow in have a unique relationship. Soil holds air, water and nutrients. Plant roots depend on these resources while using the soil to hold themselves upright. The soil in turn benefits from plant roots breaking down large clumps while preventing erosion by binding together small particles and by reducing the amount of exposed surface. When plants die and break down, they add organic nutrients to the soil and feed beneficial microorganisms.

Soil is made up of particles of varying sizes. Sand particles are the largest. Water drains quickly from sandy soil, and nutrients tend to get washed away. Sandy soil does not compact easily because the large particles leave air pockets between them. Clay particles are the smallest. Clay holds the most nutrients, but it also compacts easily, leaving little air space. Clay is slow to absorb water and equally slow to let it drain. Silt is midway between sand and clay in particle size. Most soils are a combination of these three particle sizes and are called loams.

Another aspect of soil to consider is the pH, the scale on which acidity or alkalinity is measured. The pH of soil influences the availability of nutrients; most plants prefer a pH between 5.5 and 7.5. Soil pH varies a great deal from place to place. You can buy

Poppies prefer a sandy soil.

prefer a pH that varies greatly from that of your garden soil, use planters or raised beds, where it is easier to control the pH level.

Water drainage is affected by the terrain in your garden as well as soil structure. Plants that prefer well-drained soil and do not require a lot of moisture grow well in a hillside garden with rocky soil. Water retention in these areas can be improved through the addition of organic matter. Plants that thrive on a consistent water supply or in boggy conditions are ideal for low-lying areas that retain water for longer periods or that hardly drain at all. In extremely wet areas, you can improve drainage by adding gravel, creating raised beds or using or drainage tile.

Exposure

Your garden is exposed to wind, heat, cold and rain. Some plants are better adapted than others to withstand the potential damage from these forces. Buildings, walls, fences, hills, hedges, trees and even tall perennials influence and often reduce exposure.

testing kits at most garden centres. Soil can be made more alkaline by adding horticultural lime or wood ashes, and more acidic by adding sulphur, peat moss or pine needles; however, altering soil pH can take years. If you want to grow plants that

Blueberries (below) prefer acidic soil, while strawberries (above) like alkaline soil.

Marigolds thrive in exposed locations.

Wind and heat are the elements most likely to cause damage. The sun can be intense, and heat can rise quickly on a sunny afternoon. In windy locations, plants may not be able to draw water out of the soil fast enough to replace the water lost through their leaves. Hanging baskets are especially susceptible. Choose edibles that tolerate or even thrive in hot weather for your garden's most exposed spots. Watch for wilting, and water regularly.

Too much rain can damage plants, as can overwatering. Early in the season, a light mulch will help prevent seeds or seedlings from being washed away in heavy rain. Most established plants beaten down by heavy rain will recover, but some are slower to do so. Waterlogged soil can encourage root rot because many edible plants prefer well-drained soil.

Preparing the Garden

We encourage you to garden organically, particularly in your kitchen garden. When harvesting edibles is the end goal, it's always best to use healthy gardening practices.

Take the time to properly prepare your garden soil to save yourself time and effort throughout summer. First loosen the soil and remove as many weeds as possible. Then amend the soil with organic matter.

Organic matter is a small but important component of soil. It increases the water- and nutrient-holding capacity of sandy soil. It improves clay soil by loosening it and allowing air and water to penetrate. Some of the best organic additives are

Rhubarb leaves make excellent compost mulch.

There are many types of composters on the market.

compost, well-rotted manure and composted bark or mulch. Add enough to cover your garden with a 5–10 centimetre layer, and work it in with a garden fork.

Avoid working the soil when it is very wet or very dry because you will damage the soil structure by breaking down the pockets that hold air and water, which also makes it difficult for roots to grow.

For container gardens, always use a good quality potting soil. Regular garden soil quickly loses its structure in pots, compacting into a solid mass that drains poorly. Many perennial plants can grow in the same container without any fresh potting soil for five or six years.

Compost

Compost is one of the best organic amendments for garden soil. In natural environments, compost is created when leaves, plant bits and other debris are broken down on the soil surface. This process will also take place in your garden beds if you work fresh organic matter into the soil. However, microorganisms that break down organic matter use the same nutrients as your plants. The tougher the organic matter, the more nutrients in the

soil will be used trying to break the matter down, thus robbing your plants of vital nutrients, particularly nitrogen. Also, fresh organic matter and garden debris might encourage or introduce pests and diseases to your garden.

A compost pile or bin, which can be built or bought, creates a controlled environment where organic matter can be fully broken down before being introduced into your garden. Composting is a simple

An assortment of compostable materials

An example of a vermicomposting setup

introduce beneficial microorganisms. If the pile seems very dry, sprinkle on some water—the compost should be moist but not soaking wet.

Don't put diseased or pest-ridden materials into your compost pile, or those problems could spread throughout your garden. Also do not add dog or cat feces, fats, dairy or meat; they will attract pests and smell. However, egg shells, coffee grounds and filters, tea bags, fish bones, shrimp shells and lint are all beneficial additions.

Every week or two, turn the pile over or poke holes into it. Aerating the material will speed up decomposition. A compost pile that is kept aerated can generate enough heat to destroy weed seeds and kill many damaging organisms but not usually enough to kill beneficial organisms.

process. Vegetable kitchen scraps, grass clippings and fall leaves will slowly break down if left in a pile. You can speed up the process by following a few simple guidelines.

Layer dry matter with fresh materials in your compost pile, with a larger proportion of dry matter such as chopped straw, shredded leaves or sawdust. Fresh green matter, such as vegetable scraps, grass clippings or pulled weeds, breaks down quickly and produces nitrogen, which feeds the decomposer organisms while they break down the tougher dry matter. Mix in small amounts of soil from your garden or previously finished compost to

Your compost is ready to be mixed into your garden beds when you can no longer recognize the matter that you put into it, and the temperature no longer rises upon turning. Getting to this point can take as little as one month.

For gardeners who don't have the space for an outdoor composter, vermicomposting may be the answer. This indoor method uses worms kept in a bin and is a great way to reduce your waste and create nutrient-rich compost for your container garden. Compost can also be purchased from most garden centres.

Finished compost is an invaluable garden additive.

Selecting Edible Plants

Many gardeners consider the trip to the local garden centre to choose their plants an important rite of spring, and many garden centres offer a few basic edible plants. Other gardeners find it rewarding to start their plants from seed. Both methods have benefits, and you might want to use a combination of the two. Purchasing plants can be expensive but provides you with plants that are well grown, which is useful if you don't have the room or the facilities to start seeds indoors. Some seeds require conditions that are difficult to achieve inside, or they have erratic germination rates, which makes starting them yourself impractical. However, starting from seed offers you a far greater selection of species and varieties because seed catalogues often list many more plants than are offered at garden centres. Starting from seed is discussed beginning on page 36.

When browsing through a seed catalogue, you may find references to hybrid and heirloom seeds. Hybrids are generally newer varietals of plants that have been bred for specific traits such as flavour, size, disease resistance or improved storability. These rarely grow true to type from collected seed. Heirloom refers to plant varietals that have been cultivated for generations. Some of the most intriguing vegetable selections are heirlooms, and many advocates claim the vegetables to be among the tastiest and most pest and disease resistant. Seeds can be collected from the plants, and offspring will grow true to type.

Purchased plants are sold in pots or bare-root, usually packed in moist peat moss or sawdust. Potted plants have likely been raised in the pot they are being sold in.

Bare-root plants are typically dormant, though some of the previous year's growth may be evident, or new growth may be starting—and sometimes the piece of root appears to have no evident growth, past or present. Both potted and bare-root forms are good buys, but you still need to ensure that you are getting the best quality plant for your money.

Bare-root plants are most commonly sold through mail order, but some are available in garden centres, usually in spring. When possible, choose roots that are dormant (without top growth). A plant already growing may have too little energy to recover after growing in the stressful conditions of a plastic bag.

Potted plants come in many sizes of containers, including divided cell-packs. Plants in individual pots are usually well established and generally have plenty of

There are pros and cons to starting edible plants from seed.

Do not purchase a root-bound plant.

Select plants that seem to be a good size for the container they are in. Check for roots emerging from the holes at the bottom of the cells, or gently remove the plant from the pot to look at the roots. If the roots are wrapped around the inside of the container in a thick web, the plant is too mature for the container. The plants should be compact and have good colour. Unhealthy leaves may be wilted, chewed or discoloured; tall, leggy plants have likely been deprived of light. Both root-bound and sickly plants should be avoided.

Once you get your plants home, water them if they are dry. Plants growing in small containers may require water more than once a day. Begin to harden off the plants so they can be transplanted into the garden as soon as possible. Your plants are probably accustomed to growing in the sheltered environment of a greenhouse, and they will need to become accustomed to the outdoors. Placing them out in a lightly shaded spot each day and bringing them in to a sheltered porch, garage or house each night for about a week will acclimatize them to your garden.

space for root growth, but they can be quite expensive. Plants grown in cell-packs are often inexpensive and easy to transport, but because each cell is quite small, it doesn't take long for a plant to become root-bound.

Many garden centres offer a good selection of edible plants.

Planting Edible Plants

Once your plants have hardened off, it is time to plant them out. If your beds and containers are already prepared, you are ready to start. Be sure to set aside enough time to do the job, and try to choose an overcast day for planting to help keep the plants from drying out.

The quickest way to plan out placement of your plants is to put them on the bed or in the container, mixing textures and plants as you please. Keep the tallest plants towards the back and smallest plants towards the front. Plant a small section at a time if you have a large bed to plant, or one container at a time. Leave enough room for the plants to spread. If you are adding just a few plants to accent your existing garden, plant in random clusters of three to five that will add colour, interest and impact.

Cell-pack and small-potted plants are the easiest to plant. Push on the bottom of the cell or pot with your thumb to ease the plant out. If you must handle the plant, hold it by a leaf to avoid crushing the stems. Remove and discard any damaged leaves or growth. If the rootball is densely matted and twisted, break apart the tangles to encourage the roots to extend and grow outward. Insert your trowel into the soil and pull it toward you, creating a wedge.

Plan out plant placement before you start digging.

Place your plant into the hole and firm the soil around it with your hands. Water gently but thoroughly.

Plants in large containers can be planted as described above, except that they require a larger planting hole. In a prepared bed, dig a hole about the width and depth of the pot. In most cases, you should try to get the crown at or just above soil level and loosen the surrounding soil in the planting hole. Place your plant in the hole and fill the hole in gradually, settling the soil with water as you go.

If the beds haven't been prepared, or if you are adding just one or two plants and don't want to prepare the entire bed, dig a hole twice as wide and deep as the rootball. Add a trowel full of peat moss and compost or a mycorrizae-based product to the planting hole and mix it into the garden soil before adding the plant.

Plants started in peat pots and peat pellets can be planted pot and all. When planting peat pots into the garden, remove the top 3 to 5 centimetres of the pot. If any of the pot is sticking up out of the soil, it can wick moisture away from your plant.

Bare-root plants need to be planted sooner than potted plants because they dehydrate quickly out of soil. Soak the roots in lukewarm water, and either plant them directly in the garden or into pots until they can be

Planting edibles grown in cell-packs or small containers is a fairly simple process.

Trees and shrubs, including cherries, require a larger planting hole to accommodate their rootball.

moved to the garden. Sometimes it's hard to tell the top from the bottom of bare-root plants. If you can't tell, lay the root in the soil on its side, and the plant will send the roots down and the shoots up.

A few plants are sold as bulbs, such as garlic and onion sets, which can be planted about three times as deep as the bulb is high.

More detailed planting instructions are given, as needed, in the plant accounts.

Bulbs usually need to be planted deeper than other plants.

Caring for Your Kitchen Garden

Many edible plants require little care, but all will benefit from a few maintenance basics. Regular weeding, mulching and deadheading, for example, all minimize major work.

Weeding

Controlling weed populations keeps the garden healthy and neat. Weeding may not be anyone's favourite task, but it is essential. Weeds compete with plants for light, nutrients and space; they can also harbour pests and diseases.

Weeds can be pulled by hand or with a hoe. Shortly after a rainfall, when the soil is soft and damp, is the easiest time to pull

Pull weeds so they don't crowd out your edibles.

weeds. A hoe scuffed quickly across the soil surface will uproot small weeds and sever larger ones from their roots. Try to pull weeds out while they are still small. Once they are large enough to flower, many will quickly set seed; then you will have an entire new generation to worry about.

Mulching

A layer of mulch around your plants is an excellent way to suppress weeds and also helps maintain consistent soil temperatures and retain moisture. In areas that receive heavy wind or rainfall, mulch can prevent erosion. Organic mulches such as compost, bark chips, grass clippings or shredded leaves add nutrients to the soil as they break down, thus improving the quality of the soil and, ultimately, the health of

Use mulch to control weeds and conserve water.

Use soaker hoses to conserve water.

your plants. Mulching is effective in both garden beds and planters.

Spread about 5 centimetres of mulch over the soil after you have finished planting, or spread your mulch first and then make spaces to plant afterward. Make sure the mulch is not piled thickly around the crowns and stems of your plants. Mulch that is too close to plants traps moisture, prevents air circulation and encourages fungal disease. Replenish your mulch as it breaks down over summer. A fresh layer of mulch up to 10 centimetres thick, consisting of dry material such as straw, pine needles, shredded bark or leaves, is good winter protection, particularly if you can't depend on snow to cover your garden all winter.

Watering

Water thoroughly but infrequently, making sure the water penetrates deeply into the soil. Plants given a light sprinkle of water every day develop roots that stay close to the soil surface, making the plants more vulnerable to heat and dry spells. Plants given a deep watering once a week develop a deeper root system. During a dry spell, they will be adapted to seeking out water trapped deep in the ground.

Watering deeply but infrequently applies to established or rooted plants only, not to seeds, young seedlings or new transplants. Seeds need to be kept consistently moist while germinating, and seedlings and new transplants need consistent moisture as their root systems become established. Once they're rooted in and growing well, you can water more deeply and less frequently. Use mulch to prevent water from evaporating out of the soil, and water early in the morning, if possible.

Plants in hanging baskets and other planters will probably need to be watered more frequently than plants in the ground—even twice daily during hot, sunny weather. The smaller the container, the more often the plants will need watering. However, too much water causes root rot. Dig your finger into the soil around the plant to see if it is dry.

An assortment of organic fertilizers (above) appropriate for use on edibles such as tomatoes (below).

Fertilizing

We demand a lot of growth and production from many of our edible plants; annuals in particular are expected to grow to maturity and provide us with a good crop of fruit or vegetables, all in one season.

They, in return, demand sun, nutrients and water. Mixing plenty of compost into the soil is a good start, but fertilizing regularly can make a big difference when it comes time to harvest your crop, especially if your plants are growing in containers.

Whenever possible, use organic fertilizers because they are usually less concentrated and less likely to burn the roots of your plants. They can also improve the soil as they feed your plants. Your local garden centre should carry organic fertilizers.

Fertilizer comes in many forms. Liquids or water-soluble powders are easiest to use when watering. Slow-release pellets or granules can be mixed into the garden or potting soil or sprinkled around the plant and left to work over summer. Follow the directions carefully—using too much fertilizer can kill your plants by burning their roots and may upset the microbial balance of the soil, allowing pathogens to move in or dominate.

Deadheading

Deadheading is the removal of flowers once they have finished blooming. It keeps plants looking tidy, prevents the plant from spreading seeds (and therefore seedlings), often prolongs blooming and helps prevent pest and disease problems.

Deadhead calendula to keep more flowers coming.

Deadheading is not necessary for every plant. Some plants with seed heads are left in place so the seeds can ripen and be collected in fall, or to provide interest in the garden over winter. Other plants are short-lived, and leaving some of the seed heads in place encourages future generations to replace the old plants.

Pinch dead flowers off by hand or snip them off with hand pruners. Prune back bushy plants that have many tiny flowers, particularly ones such as thyme that have a short bloom period, more aggressively with garden shears once they have finished flowering. Shearing will promote new growth and possibly blooms later in the season.

Arugula is a prolific self-seeder.

Leave coriander's seed heads in place to ripen.

Basil will benefit from pinching.

Pruning

Resilient health, plentiful blooming and compact growth are signs of a well-groomed garden. The methods for pruning are simple, but experiment to get it right.

Thin out clump-forming perennials such as beebalm early in the year when the shoots first emerge. The clump of stems allows little air or light into the centre of the plant, and removing half of the early shoots will increase air circulation and prevent diseases such as powdery mildew.

The increased light encourages more compact growth and more flowers. Throughout the growing season, remove any growth that is weak, diseased or growing in the wrong direction.

Trimming or pinching plants is a simple procedure, but timing it correctly and achieving just the right look can be tricky. Early in the year, before the flower buds have appeared, trim the plant to encourage new side shoots. Going stem by stem, remove the tip and some stem of the plant just above a leaf or pair of leaves. If you have a lot of plants, you can trim off the tops with your hedge shears to one-third of the height you expect the plants to reach.

Give plants enough time to set buds and flower. Don't pinch back or prune most spring-flowering plants, or they will not flower. Early summer or midsummer bloomers should be pinched or pruned only once, as early in the season as possible. Late summer and fall bloomers can be pinched several times, but leave them alone after June. Don't pinch or prune a plant if flower buds have formed; it may not have enough energy or time left in the year to develop a new set of buds.

Raspberries will need seasonal pruning to keep them tidy and productive.

Peas will benefit from a vertical support.

Staking and Supports

A few plants need some support to look their best. Three basic types of stakes go with different growth habits. Tall plants may need to be tied to a strong, narrow pole or forked branch pushed into the

Unsupported sunflowers may blow over in a strong wind.

ground beside them. Top-heavy plants benefit from a wire hoop—a tomato cage or a peony ring. Plants with floppy tangles of stems can be supported with twiggy branches inserted into the ground around the young plants that then grow up into the twigs.

To reduce the need for staking, avoid using a richer soil than is recommended. Also, a plant that likes full sun will be stretched out and leggy if grown in the shade. Mix in plants that have a more stable structure between those that need support. A floppy plant may still fall over slightly, but only as far as its neighbour will allow. Many plants are available in compact varieties that don't require staking.

Climbing plants will all benefit from some kind of support. Fences, trellises, arbours, pergolas and walls can all be used. Some vines will naturally twine around a structure, some will attach themselves to the structure with tendrils, aerial rootlets or suction cups, and some will need to be attached to the structure with soft ties. Ensure that the support is sturdy enough to handle the weight of the plant.

Extending the Growing Season

Frost is the almighty threat we face as gardeners. It determines whether the season will continue or not. However, there are ways to protect plants to extend your growing season by days, weeks, even months, depending on the strategy you use. Sometimes it is as simple as moving containers to a sheltered spot or covering garden plants with a sheet if frost threatens. Other methods include cold frames, cloches and greenhouses.

Cold air tends to move downward to the lowest point, following the slopes in hills, walls and so on. The cool air will pool around anything that prevents it from moving any farther, such as a grouping of plants or a structure. Plants are better prepared to ward off any exposure to that cold air or to frost in spring if they've been

Cold frames (above) and cloches (below) are excellent tools for extending the growing season.

hardened off. Harden off plants started indoors by gradually acclimating them to outside conditions by setting them in a sheltered location outdoors for increasing lengths of time over a period of days.

Cold frames are used to protect young plants grown from seeds or cuttings. A cold frame is a small structure with a slanted glass or plexi-glass lid, often built close to the ground. It acts like a mini greenhouse by allowing the light to penetrate for plant growth and to heat the inside of the structure. The top is built to open fully for access to the plants, but it can also be opened just slightly throughout the day to prevent the plants from becoming too warm and to slowly harden off the plants inside to the temperatures outside.

Cloches serve the same purpose as cold frames, but whereas cold frames protect groups of plants, cloches are meant for individual plants. They are often bell-shaped and made of blown, thickened glass for longevity, but I've also seen plastic versions that are much less expensive and easier to store. A cloche can even be homemade; simply cut the bottom from a plastic water or pop bottle and place the bottle over top of the seedling. The lid can be left on at night and removed during the day, allowing the air to move freely in and out while the plant acclimates to outside temperatures. Later on the neck of the bottle can be cut away, leaving only a plastic cylinder around the base of the plant to protect it from chewing insects as well as to act as a support throughout the growing season. Or the bottle can be taken away all together.

Greenhouses are a world unto their own. With a greenhouse, regardless of size, you can extend your season by weeks or months, or you can just garden year-round. A greenhouse provides the best protection from the outdoor elements and is invaluable to gardeners in regions with short summers and cold winters. Plants can be raised from seed to maturity at any time of year, or they can be started in the greenhouse and moved to cold frames before they're planted outdoors for the duration of the growing season.

Make your own garden cloches using plastic bottles.

Overwintering Plants in Containers

Many edible perennial plants can be grown in pots rather than in the ground. Some invasive herbs such as mint are good choices for containers because their spread is controlled, and they are very hardy. Or maybe you just don't want to let your lack of in-ground garden space keep you from enjoying delicious rhubarb every summer.

Overwintering perennials, even hardy ones, in containers can be a challenge because plants in containers are more susceptible to winter damage than plants in the garden. To get container plants through a tough Canadian winter, simply move the containers to a sheltered spot such as an unheated garage, enclosed porch or garden shed. Basement window wells are also good places to overwinter containers: they are sheltered, below ground and receive some heat from the window. Layer straw at the bottom of the well, sit your pots on the straw, and then cover them with more straw. Wait until the soil in the pots has frozen to discourage mice that might make their home in the straw from eating the roots, and to prevent root rot.

The pots themselves can be weatherproofed before you plant them—highrise dwellers with balcony gardens might consider weatherproofing pots too, even for their annuals. Put a layer of insulation at the bottom and around the inside of the pot before you add soil and plants. Just make sure that excess water can still drain freely from the container. Insulation will pull double duty, helping keep plants cool in summer as well as protecting them in winter.

Overwintering Tender Perennials

Many plants grown as annuals in Canada are actually perennials or shrubs that are native to warmer climates and unable to survive our cold winters; others are

Even hardy perennials need winter protection when grown in containers.

ground freezes. Shake the loose dirt away let the roots dry out in a cool, dark place. Once dry, dust them with an anti-fungal powder and store them in moist peat moss or coarse sawdust. Keep them in a dark, dry place that is cold but doesn't freeze. If they start to sprout, pot them and keep them in moist soil in a bright window. Pot them up in late winter or early spring, whether they have started sprouting or not, so they will be ready for spring planting.

Bring tender perennials such as rosemary (left) and bay laurel (below) indoors over winter.

biennials. You can use several techniques to keep these plants for more than one summer.

Some tropical perennials can simply be brought inside and treated as houseplants in the colder months. Use a reverse hardening-off process to acclimatize plants to an indoor environment. Plants that are grown in the sun all summer should be gradually moved to shady garden spots. They will develop more efficient leaves that are capable of surviving in the comparatively limited light indoors.

Perennial plants with tuberous roots can be dug up, stored over winter and replanted in spring. Dig up the roots in fall after the plant dies back but before the

Propagation

Learning to propagate your own plants is an interesting and challenging aspect of gardening that can save you money, but it also takes time and space. Seeds, cuttings and divisions are the three methods of increasing your plant population.

Seeds

Seed catalogues from different growers offer many types and varieties of edible plants. Other places to find seeds include the internet, local garden centres and seed exchange groups. Starting your own plants can save you money, particularly if you want a lot of plants. The basic equipment is not expensive, and most seeds can be started in a sunny window. However, you may run out of room if you start with more than one or two trays. That is why many gardeners start a few specialty plants indoors but buy most plants from a garden centre. Each plant in this book has specific information on starting it from seed, if any is required, but a few basic steps can be followed for all seeds.

The easiest way to start seeds is in cell-packs in trays with plastic dome covers. The cell-packs keep roots separated, and the tray and dome keep moisture in. Seeds can also be started in pots, peat pots or peat pellets. The advantage to starting in peat pots or pellets is that you will not disturb the roots when you transplant.

Fill your pots or seed trays with a sterile soil mix that is intended for seedlings. Firm it down slightly, but not too firmly or it will not drain well. Wet the soil before planting your seeds to prevent them from getting washed around.

Starting plants indoors from seed requires time and space but can be rewarding.

Plant only one type of seed per pot or flat. Large seeds can be planted one or two to a cell, but place smaller seeds in a folded piece of paper and sprinkle them evenly over the soil surface. Very tiny seeds can be mixed with fine sand and then sprinkled on the soil surface. These small seeds do not need to be covered with any more soil, but lightly cover other seeds unless they need to be exposed to light to germinate; in that case, leave the seeds on the soil surface regardless of their size.

Place pots or flats of seeds in plastic bags to retain humidity while the seeds are germinating. Many planting trays come with clear plastic covers that keep in the moisture. Remove the covers once the seeds have germinated, and place the trays or pots in a bright location out of direct sun. Mist the soil with water if it starts to dry out.

All seedlings are susceptible to "damping off," caused by soil-borne fungi. An afflicted seedling will appear to have been pinched at soil level. The pinched area blackens, and the seedling topples over and dies. Sterile soil mix, evenly moist soil and good air circulation will help prevent this problem.

Seeds provide all the energy and nutrients that young seedlings require. Small seedlings do not need to be fertilized until they have about four or five true leaves. When the first leaves that sprouted begin to shrivel, the plant has used up all its seed energy, and you can begin to use a fertilizer diluted to one-quarter.

If the seedlings get too big for their containers before you are ready to plant out, you may have to "up-pot" them to prevent them from becoming root-bound. Harden off plants by exposing them to outdoor

Seed-starting supplies (below left); pot up seedlings until they can be planted outside (below right).

Beets can be sown directly into the garden.

conditions for longer every day for at least a week before planting them out.

Some seeds can be planted directly in the garden. The procedure is similar to that of starting seeds indoors. Begin with a well-prepared bed that has been raked smooth. The small furrows left by the rake help hold moisture and prevent the seeds from being washed away. Sprinkle the seeds onto the soil and cover them lightly with peat moss or more soil. Larger seeds can be planted slightly deeper. Very tiny seeds can be mixed with sand for more even sowing. Keep the soil moist to ensure even germination. Use a gentle spray to avoid washing the seeds around the bed because they inevitably pool into dense clumps.

Cover your newly seeded bed with chicken wire, an old sheet or some thorny branches to discourage pets from digging.

Large seeds are easy to space out well when you sow them. With small seeds, you may find that the new plants need to be thinned out to give adjacent plants room to grow properly. Pull out the weaker plants when groups look crowded. Some are edible and can be used as spring greens in a salad or steamed as a side dish.

Cuttings

Cuttings are an excellent way to propagate varieties and cultivars that don't come true from seed or don't produce seed at all. Each cutting will grow into a reproduction of the parent plant. Cuttings are taken from the stems of some plants and the roots of others.

Stem Cuttings

Stem cuttings are generally taken in spring and early summer when plants are busy growing and are full of the right hormones to promote quick root growth. Don't take cuttings from plants that are in flower; they are busy reproducing.

Cuttings need to be kept in a warm, humid place to root, which makes them very prone to fungal diseases. Provide a clean, sterile environment and encourage quick rooting to increase the survival rate of your cuttings.

Stripping leaves from cutting (top); dipping cutting in rooting hormone (centre); and planting cutting (bottom).

Determine the size of cuttings by the number of leaf nodes on the cutting. You will want at least three or four nodes (where the leaf joins the stem). The base of the cutting should be just below a node. Always use a sharp, sterile knife to make the cuttings. Cut straight across the stem.

Strip the leaves gently from the lower half of the cutting, and dip the end of the cutting into rooting-hormone powder. Plant cuttings in a tray of moist, sterile soil mix, leaving the half still with leaves above soil level, and keep them in a warm place in bright, indirect light.

Most cuttings require one to four weeks to root. Plants with several nodes close together often root quickly and abundantly. New growth is a good sign that your cutting has rooted. Some gardeners leave the cuttings alone until they can see roots through the holes in the bottoms of the pots.

Once your cuttings have rooted, pot them up individually in a sterile potting soil and keep them in a sheltered area or cold frame and until they are large enough to plant in the garden. They may need some protection over the first winter.

Horseradish (above) is easy to propagate by root cuttings; beebalm (below) can be propagated by basal cuttings.

Basal Cuttings

Many plants send up new shoots or plantlets around their bases. Basal cuttings involve removing the new growth from the main clump and rooting it in the same manner as stem cuttings. Often, the plantlets will already have a few roots growing. The young plants develop quickly and may even grow to flowering size the first summer.

Root Cuttings

The main difference between root cuttings and stem cuttings is that the root cuttings must be kept fairly dry because they can rot easily.

Take cuttings from the fleshy roots of certain plants in early or mid-spring when the roots are just about to break dormancy. At this time, the roots are full of nutrients the plants stored the previous summer and fall, and hormones are initiating growth.

Use a sterile knife to cut the root into pieces 2.5 to 5 centimetres long. Remove any side roots. Keep track of which end is up. Roots must be planted in a vertical position in the soil, in the orientation they held while attached to the parent plant. Plant the sections in a sterile soil mix in pots or planting trays, leaving a tiny bit of the top poking up out of the soil.

Tarragon will need to be divided every few years.

Keep the cuttings in a warm place out of direct sunlight, and don't over water. The plants will send up new shoots once they have rooted. They can then be planted in the same manner as rooted stem cuttings.

The easiest root cuttings to propagate are rhizomes. Take rhizome cuttings when the plant is growing vigorously (usually in late spring or early summer). Dig up a section of rhizome and cut it into pieces, with a node in each piece. Lay the rhizome pieces flat on top of some sterile, moist soil and almost cover them with more soil mix. Once your cuttings are established, pot them individually.

Division

Division is quite possibly the easiest way to propagate most perennials. Trees, shrubs and other woody perennials, including some vines, cannot be divided because they share a central stem or crown.

Most herbaceous perennials form larger and larger clumps as they grow. Dividing this clump will rejuvenate the plant, keep its size in check and provide more plants. Some plants need dividing almost every year to keep them vigorous, while others can last a few years before dividing. You will know a plant should be divided if:

- the centre of the plant dies out
- the plant no longer flowers as profusely as it did in previous years
- the plant encroaches on the growing space of other plants in the bed.

Dig up the entire plant and knock any large clods of soil away from the rootball, then split the clump into several pieces. A small plant with fibrous roots can be torn into sections by hand. A large plant can be pried apart with a pair of garden forks. Plants with thicker tuberous or rhizomatous roots can be cut into sections with a sharp, sterile knife.

In all cases, cut away any dead parts and replant only the newer, more vigorous divisions, working quickly to prevent the exposed roots from drying out. Put one or two of them into the original location after working organic matter into the soil first. Move the other divisions to new spots in the garden, or pot them and give them away. Water new transplants thoroughly.

The larger the section, the more quickly the plant will re-establish itself. Newly planted divisions need regular watering and, for the first few days, shade from direct sunlight. A light covering of burlap or damp newspaper should suffice for this short period. Move divisions that have been planted in pots to the shade.

Some gardeners prefer to divide plants while they are dormant, and others prefer to divide them while they are growing vigorously. If you do divide plants while they are growing, cut back one-third to one-half of the growth so as not to stress the roots while they are repairing the damage.

Dig up a plant that needs dividing (top); once you have the rootball (centre), pull it into sections for replanting (bottom).

Harvesting Your Kitchen Garden

For most kitchen gardeners, the delight is in the harvest. Each plant featured in this book will have suggestions of when to harvest, but here are a few general tips.

Make a list of the maturity dates for the edible plants you're growing. Once the time allowance has been met, observe the plants to see if they're ready to be harvested. Don't harvest too early or too late. Vegetables and fruits picked earlier than necessary are often bland, hard and small; left too long, they are often bland, tough and stringy. Only trial and error will teach you when the perfect time to harvest is, but observe and taste your produce and record your findings to better prepare for the next growing season.

Many leaves, including leafy vegetables and herbs, can be harvested throughout the growing season, or all year when grown either in a climate that allows it or indoors. However, the window of opportunity for some leafy vegetables, such as lettuce, spinach, arugula and mustard greens, is small. Pick them early in the season or they become bitter and unusable, and pick just the amount you need for one sitting, rather than picking them all at once. Once they're past their prime, pull them up and re-seed for an additional crop.

Depending on the size of the plant and how much lush growth is produced, pinch out growth for use on a regular basis. Pinch leaves from the most tender parts of

Harvest spinach (below left) and lettuce (below right) early in the season for the best flavour.

Pick nasturtiums for fresh use all season.

For the best culinary experience, try to harvest right before preparing, cooking or eating the produce to get the full benefit of the flavour and nutrients. However, if you're planning on storing leafy vegetables and herbs for any length of time, harvest early in the morning, preferably a cool morning. Wait until the dew evaporates but before it gets too hot. Waiting one or two days after a thorough watering is also best, so the leaves are plump and bursting with essential oils. Place the stems in a little water and refrigerate for a few hours before cleaning and processing for storage.

Flowers that are used fresh can be picked throughout their blooming cycle, but they do vary somewhat as to peak harvesting times. For example, chamomile flowers should be picked when they're fully open, and others are better harvested just before they open.

the plant, avoiding the woody portions unless you plan on discarding them later. Don't take too much at a time, but if a hard shearing is necessary to perk up the plant, go ahead—it won't hurt the plant's longevity.

Use sharp, clean tools when harvesting fruits and vegetables. Some plants can be damaged when the fruit is pulled off rather than cut off with a sharp tool, which may result in a plant that is no longer able to

Take care when pulling tomatoes from the vine.

Radishes are a fast-maturing root crop.

produce. Pulling on a tomato and snapping your tomato plant in half early on will be the season's biggest disappointment, particularly because it could have been prevented.

Usually seeds are harvested once they've turned colour, often from green to brown, and usually in fall. For plants with seeds that spill all over the ground once they've ripened, place a small paper bag over the seed head shortly before the seeds ripen. Gently cinch the mouth of the bag to the stem without cutting into the stem. Once the seeds have ripened, cut the stem where the bag is attached. If the seeds require a drying period, dry them in the bag and store them in an airtight container later.

Root vegetables are harvested mostly in fall, once the growing season is finished— quick-growing radishes are an exception. Harvesting roots is as simple as digging them up. Remove the entire root of annuals when you're doing your fall cleanup.

For hardy plants that you intend to leave in the ground, such as sunchokes and horseradish, remove no more than one-third of the root and leave the rest. Gently rinse the soil off and let the roots dry before further processing.

Dig bulbs such as onions and garlic either in late summer or early fall, depending on when you planted them.

Drying Edible Plants

Fresh is always best, but when you have more produce than you can eat fresh, or you want to have some available for those cold winter months, there are several methods of preservation. Freezing is probably the easiest and most common method for certain fruits and vegetables, such as berries and legumes. However, drying is an excellent preservation method for most herbs, seeds and flowers.

It is important to ensure that all of the moisture is removed from fresh leaves. You need a location with adequate air circulation and enough space. Most gardeners collect a handful of leafy stems, tie the stems together in a bunch and hang them upside down until crackly dry to the

Amaranth seeds will ripen in fall.

Dry herbs such as dill (above) and flowers such as roses (below) to preserve them for later use.

touch. To preserve the colour of your herbs, dry them in a dark place. The length of drying time will differ from one plant to another. Once dried, separate the bundles and gently strip the leaves from the stems. Larger leaves that have already been separated from the stems can be crumbled into pieces for storing.

Cut large flower heads such as roses from their stems. Separate the petals and loosely spread them out to dry. Some flowers can be dried whole, such as calendula. The petals can be separated later, once dried. Other flowers are best dried in bunches, loosely tied with string. Cover the flower heads with paper bags while drying to catch petals if they fall. Depending on what you're using the flowers for, either leave them left intact once dry or strip them from the stems just as you would the leaves. Store your dried herbs and flowers in airtight containers in a dark, cool place to preserve their colours and flavours.

Seeds are easiest to dry when you cut the stem with the flower head attached and store the entire cluster in a paper bag until dry, shaking them loose later on. Once the seeds are dry, store them in labelled, airtight containers.

Problems and Pests

Pests and diseases may attack your kitchen garden from time to time. Integrated Pest (or Plant) Management (IPM) is a moderate approach to dealing with them. The goal of IPM is to reduce problems so only negligible damage is done. You must determine what degree of damage is acceptable to you. Consider whether the damage is localized or covers an entire plant. Will the pest or disease kill the plant or is it affecting only the outward appearance? Attempting to totally eradicate pests is futile.

IPM includes learning about your plants and the conditions they need for healthy growth. It is also useful to learn which pests might affect your plants, where and when to look for those pests and how to control them. Keep records of pest damage because your observations can reveal patterns useful in spotting recurring problems and in planning your maintenance regime.

Prevention and Control

New annual edible plants are planted each spring, and you may choose to plant different species each year. These factors make it difficult for pests and diseases to find their preferred host plants and establish a population. However, because many edibles are closely related, any

Aphids (below) and powdery mildew (above) are common garden problems.

problems that set in over summer are likely to attack all the plants in the same family.

There are four levels of effective and responsible pest management. Cultural controls are the most important, followed by physical controls and biological controls. Resort to chemical controls only when the first three possibilities have been exhausted.

Cultural controls are the gardening techniques you use in the day-to-day care of your garden. The first line of defence against pests and diseases is to prevent them from attacking in the first place. If certain plants are prone to problems, choose resistant varieties. Grow plants in the conditions they prefer and keep your soil healthy by adding plenty of organic matter. Space the plants so that they have good air circulation around them and are not stressed by competing for light, nutrients and space. Take plants that are destroyed by the same pests every year out of the landscape. Remove and dispose of diseased foliage and branches, and prevent the spread of disease by keeping gardening tools clean and by tidying up fallen leaves and dead plant matter at the end of every growing season. Remember: healthy plants can fend for themselves and sustain some damage, but stressed or weakened plants are more prone to attack.

Physical controls are generally used to combat insect and animal pests. They include picking insects off plants by hand, traps, barriers, scarecrows and natural repellents that make a plant taste or smell bad to pests. Physical control of diseases usually involves removing the infected plant or parts of the plant to prevent the spread of the problem.

Biological controls use populations of natural predators that prey on pests. Birds, snakes, frogs, spiders, many insects and certain bacteria can play an important role

Ladybugs (top), ground beetles (centre) and lacewings (bottom) are all beneficial insect predators.

Some organic pesticides are derived from pyrethrum daisies.

in keeping pest populations manageable. Encourage these creatures to take up permanent residence in your garden by planting appropriate food sources and providing a welcoming habitat.

Chemical controls are a last resort. Organic pesticides are available and most garden centres. They are no less dangerous than inorganic ones, but they break down into harmless compounds. The main drawback to using any chemicals is that they will also kill the beneficial insects you have been trying to attract to your garden. Apply only in the recommended amount, only to the pests listed on the label. Proper and early identification of pests is vital to finding a quick solution.

About This Guide

The plants featured in this book are organized into nine categories based on food type: root vegetables, head and stem vegetables, fruiting vegetables, leafy greens, berries, other fruits, herbs, seeds and edible flowers. Within each category, they are organized alphabetically by their most common name. Additional common names appear as well. The botanical name is always listed after the common name.

Clearly indicated within each entry are the plant's height and spread ranges, outstanding features and hardiness zones, if applicable. Each entry gives clear instructions for starting, growing and harvesting the plants, tips on where to grow the plant, and recommends many favourite selections. If height and spread ranges are not given for every recommended plant, assume these ranges are the same as those provided in the Features section. Your local garden centre will have any additional information about the plant and will help you make your plant selections. Finally, the Problems and Pests section in each account deals with issues that may afflict your garden plants from time to time.

Beet

Beta

Features: clump-forming biennial grown as an annual; attractive, edible leaves; edible red, yellow or red-and-white-ringed root **Height:** 20–45 cm **Spread:** 10–25 cm

'Touchstone Gold'

Beets are not only delicious but also versatile. The plump, rounded or cylindrical roots are the most commonly eaten part. The tops are also edible, are incredibly nutritious and can be compared in flavour to spinach and Swiss chard. Beets and Swiss chard are closely related, both being members of the genus Beta.

Starting
The corky, wrinkled seeds are actually dry fruits that contain several tiny seeds. Plant them directly in the garden around the last frost date, 7–15 cm apart. You will probably have to thin them a bit because several plants can sprout from each fruit. Many

beets are fairly quick to mature; you can plant a second crop in midsummer for a fall harvest.

Growing
Beets grow well in **full sun** or **partial shade**. They grow best in cool weather. The soil should be **fertile, moist** and **well drained**. Mulch lightly with compost to maintain moisture and improve soil texture.

Harvesting
Beets mature in 45–80 days, depending on the variety. Short-season beets are best for immediate eating and preserving, and long-season beets are the better choice for

storing over winter. Pick beets as soon as they are big enough to eat. They are tender when young but can become woody as they mature.

You can pick beet leaves without pulling up the entire beet if you want to use them for fresh or steamed greens. Don't pull all the leaves off a beet; just remove a few at a time from any one plant.

Tips
Beets have attractive red-veined, dark green foliage. They look good in small groups in a border and make interesting edging plants. They can even be included in large mixed container plantings or on their own in smaller containers. If you have the space and enough light, beets can be grown indoors as well.

Recommended
B. vulgaris forms a dense rosette of glossy, dark green leaves, often with deep red stems and veins. There are many cultivars available. '**Alto**' produces sweet, cylindrical red roots. '**Early Wonder**' and '**Red**

Ace' are good round red cultivars. '**Bull's Blood**' matures in 45 days as a salad leaf, and 70 days for roots. '**Detroit Dark Red**' has dark red beets; '**Golden Detroit**' has red skin and yellow flesh. '**Ruby Queen**' is an early selection, ready in 48–55 days. '**Pablo**' and '**Zeppo**' are bright red, smaller beets that are good for container growing.

Popular novelty beet varieties include the white '**Albina Vereduna**,' ready for harvest in 70 days; '**Chioggia**,' an heirloom that produces red-and-white-ringed roots; and the yellow '**Touchstone Gold**,' ready for harvest is 60 days.

Problems and Pests
Beets are generally problem free, but occasional trouble with scab, root maggots and flea beetles can occur.

'Detroit Dark Red'

Never fear if you get beet juice on your clothing; it won't stain. Chemists inform us that the red molecule in beets is very large and doesn't adhere to other molecules.

Carrot

Daucus

Features: biennial grown as an annual; feathery foliage; edible root
Height: 20–45 cm **Spread:** 5–10 cm

For many years, there were no more than two or three types of carrot to grow; today there is an endless array of hybrids, cultivars and heirloom varieties. You could choose two different types each growing season for the rest of your life and never get close to growing all of them…so experiment and try something new!

Starting

Carrots can be sown directly into the garden once the last frost date has passed and the soil has warmed up. The tiny seeds are difficult to plant evenly. Mix them with sand before you sow them to spread them more evenly and reduce the need for thinning. Cover the seeds only very lightly, and keep the seedbed moist to encourage even germination.

Growing

Carrots grow best in **full sun**. The soil should be **average to fertile, well drained** and **deeply prepared**. Be sure that the soil is loose and free of rocks to a depth of 20–30 cm to give the roots plenty of room to grow. If your soil is very rocky or shallow, you may wish to plant carrots in raised beds to provide deeper, looser soil; or just grow shorter varieties of carrots.

As the carrots develop, pull a few of the more crowded ones out, leaving room for the others to fill in (the root can be eaten at all stages of development). Hill up the soil around the tops to keep them covered throughout the growing process.

Harvesting

Big, bushy tops are no indication that carrots are ready for picking. A better indication of their development is to look at the top of the carrots, just at soil level. You can pull carrots up by getting a good grip on the greens in loose enough soil, but you may need a garden fork to dig them up in heavier soil.

To keep carrots for a long time, store them in a cold, frost-free place in containers of moistened sand.

Tips

Carrots make an excellent ornamental grouping or edging plant. The feathery foliage provides an attractive background for flowers. Carrots can also be grown in containers with adequate depth for root growth, either on the patio or even indoors with enough light.

Carrots weren't originally orange. Artwork painted over 200 years ago depicts carrots in pale yellows, dark purples and reds, rather than orange.

Recommended

D. carota* var. *sativus forms a bushy mound of feathery foliage. It matures in 50–75 days. The edible roots may be orange, red, yellow, white or purple, and from long and slender to short and round. Choose a type based on flavour, how long you want to store them and how suitable your soil is. **'Bolero'** produces high yields in difficult climates. **'Napoli'** is an early-maturing, sweet carrot. **'Resistafly'** is rust fly resistant. **'Scarlet Nantes'** ('Nantes') is a popular, sweet heirloom carrot. Novelty selections include **'Atomic Red,' 'Cosmic Purple'** and **'White Satin.'** Good container selections include **'Little Finger'** and **'Parisienne,'** both of which produce baby carrots.

Problems and Pests

Carrot rust flies and root maggots can sometimes be troublesome.

Kohlrabi

Brassica

Features: biennial grown as an annual; silvery or blue-green foliage; edible bulbous stem base **Height:** 30 cm **Spread:** 30 cm

The tender, swollen stem base of kohlrabi is curious looking, like something you'd imagine would be growing in a futuristic garden. But don't let its funny appearance put you off of this yummy vegetable. The leaf bases become stretched as the bulb forms, and new leaves continue to sprout from the top of the rounded bulb. See, nothing to fear. Let the experimentation begin!

Starting
Seeds can be sown directly in the garden approximately 30 cm apart around the last frost date. This plant matures quite quickly, so make several small sowings 1–2 weeks apart to have tender, young kohlrabi for most of summer.

Growing
Kohlrabi grows best in **full sun**. The soil should be **fertile, moist** and **well drained**, though plants adapt to most moist soils. A floating row cover will keep pests off.

Harvesting
Keep a close eye on your kohlrabi because the bulbs can become tough and woody quickly if left in the ground too long. The bulbs are generally well rounded and

5–10 cm in diameter when ready for harvesting. Pull up the entire plant and cut just below the bulb. Then cut the leaves and stems off and compost them or use them to mulch the bed.

Tips

Low and bushy, with white or purple bulbs, kohlrabi makes an interesting edging plant for beds and borders and can be included in container gardens, particularly those in which you like to change the plantings regularly.

Recommended

B. oleracea subsp. *gongylodes* forms a low, bushy clump of blue-green foliage. As the plant matures, the stem just above ground level swells and becomes rounded. This is the edible part. '**Purple**' and '**White**' are common in seed catalogues and are the standard hybrids of the subspecies. They mature in 55 days, are very productive and are nutty in flavour

without becoming woody. '**Granlibakken**' is an early variety, ready in 46 days because of its vigour. It bears light green, uniform, rounded bulbs with a tender texture and sweet flavour. '**Korridor**' is also an early selection, bearing white bulbs with a rich flavour. '**Kolibri**' is considered to be one of the best-tasting purple varieties, ready in 45 days.

Problems and Pests

Problems with cutworms, leaf miners, caterpillars, root maggots, cabbage white butterfly larvae, white rust, downy mildew and powdery mildew can occur. Avoid planting any Brassica in the same spot in successive years.

Kohlrabi is a cross between a cabbage and a turnip, something that tends to ward off those who like neither, but it's a combination made in heaven.

Onion

Allium

Features: clumping biennial or perennial often grown as an annual; upright, tubular leaves; edible bulbs and leaves **Height:** 45–60 cm **Spread:** 5–10 cm

---

Onions have been cultivated for so long that their country of origin is not known. It is known, however, that the ancient Greeks, Romans and Egyptians all grew and ate onions in great abundance, and the onion's popularity has not waned. That's a lot to say for a vegetable that makes our eyes tear up and leaves us with bad breath.

Starting

Start seeds indoors 6–8 weeks before you plan to plant them outdoors, or sow seeds directly in the garden once the last frost date has passed; you may have to thin the seedlings to get bigger bulbs. Or, purchase and plant sets of starter onions in spring.

Bunching onions are usually started from seed sown directly in the garden. Make several smaller sowings 2–3 weeks apart from spring to midsummer for a regular supply.

Growing

Onions prefer **full sun**. The soil should be **fertile, moist** and **well drained**. Onions

'Evergreen'

use plenty of water but will rot in very wet soil. They are poor at competing with other plants, so keep them well weeded. Mulch to conserve moisture and keep the weeds down.

Harvesting

All onions can be harvested and used as needed throughout the season. For green onions, pull up onions that need thinning, or just pinch back the tops if you want the bulbs to mature or the plant to continue to produce leaves.

Bulb onions grown for storage are ready to be harvested when the leaves begin to yellow and flop over and the shoulders of the bulbs are just visible above the soil line. Pull them up and let them dry for a few days before storing them in a dry, cold, frost-free spot.

Tips

Onions have fascinating cylindrical leaves that add an interesting vertical accent to the garden. Include them in beds, borders and containers, but if you want big bulbs, don't overly crowd them with other plants.

Recommended

A. cepa (bulb onion) forms a clump of cylindrical foliage and develops a large,

Onions can be left in the ground over winter, though the flavour can become quite strong the second year. They will flower the second summer.

round or flattened bulb. Bulb formation is day-length dependent; for Canadian gardens, choose varieties developed for long days. There is a myriad of sizes, colours, flavours and textures to choose from. **'Candy'** is a vigorous, extra-early selection that bears large, mildly sweet bulbs. **'Redwing'** is ultra reliable, producing white, medium-sized onions with deep maroon skins. **'Red Bull'** maintains its dark red colour almost to its centre. **'Sweet Spanish'** bears yellow, sweet, mild bulbs. **'Walla Walla'** produces mild, sweet, large, flattened bulbs with golden skins. It is not a good keeper, so grow only a few and use them immediately after harvest.

A. fistulosum (bunching onion, green onion, scallion) forms a clump of foliage that quickly begins to divide and multiply from the base. Plants may develop small bulbs or no bulbs at all. **'Evergreen'** bears crisp, deep green, mild-tasting foliage. **'Salad Apache'** bears deep purple-red–skinned ends.

Problems and Pests

Problems with smut, onion maggots and rot can occur.

Parsnip

Pastinaca

Features: biennial grown as an annual; feathery foliage; sweet, edible root
Height: 30–45 cm **Spread:** 15–20 cm

Despite needing a fairly long season to mature, parsnips are well suited to northern gardens because they are best eaten once they have had a few good frosts to sweeten their roots. Parsnips are a lovely addition to soups and stews on cold fall days.

Starting

Sow seeds directly into the garden as soon as the soil can be worked. Be sure to keep the soil moist to ensure good germination. Seeds can be slow to germinate, sometimes taking up to 3 weeks, so mark the location where you plant them.

Growing

Parsnips grow best in **full sun** but tolerate some light shade. The soil should be of **average fertility, moist** and **well drained**. Be sure to work the soil well and mix in compost to improve the texture. Roots develop poorly in heavy soil. To avoid "hairy" roots, do not use manure as a fertilizer. However, a bed that has manure in it from the previous year should grow good parsnips in the current year.

Mulch to suppress weed growth and to conserve moisture.

Harvesting

The roots can be pulled up in fall, after the first few frosts, and stored in damp sand in a cold, frost-free location for up to 6 months. Parsnips can also be pulled from the garden all winter in areas where the ground does not freeze solid, or mulched with straw and pulled up in spring, before they sprout new growth. Frost improves the flavour because some of the root starches are converted to sugar in freezing weather.

Tips

Not the most ornamental of vegetables, parsnips provide a dark, leafy background to low-growing plants and produce plenty of vegetable for very little effort. Unlike carrots, parsnip tops are very big and spreading, so they take up a lot of room.

Recommended

P. sativa is an upright plant with dark green, divided leaves. It develops a long,

'Hollow Crown'

pale creamy yellow root that looks like a carrot. **'Andover,' 'Harris Model'** and **'Hollow Crown'** are commonly available cultivars. **'Gladiator'** is considered to be the best hybrid parsnip for its silky smooth skin, true parsnip flavour and consistently high quality. **'Arrow'** is an earlier variety producing large, uniform roots with a sweet, delicate flavour and tender texture. **'Tender & True'** is an heirloom variety bearing long, canker-resistant roots.

Problems and Pests

Canker, carrot rust flies and onion maggots can affect parsnips.

This cousin of the carrot was once prescribed as a treatment for ulcers, colic, pain, consumption, snake bites and psychological ills.

Potato

Solanum

Features: bushy annual; pink, purple or white flowers; edible tubers
Height: 45–60 cm **Spread:** 30–60 cm

Potatoes were cultivated in South America for centuries before the Spanish introduced them to Europe. They were only introduced to North America after European immigrants brought them here. Today, heirloom varieties are in fashion, mixing it up with newer cultivars fancy and plain, small and large; no matter what new varieties come out, the heirloom potatoes are often the best and have stood the test of time.

Starting

Sets of seed potatoes can be purchased and planted in spring a few weeks before the last frost date, as long as the soil isn't too cold and wet. Young plants can tolerate a light frost, but not a hard freeze. Cut the seed potatoes into smaller pieces so that each piece has an "eye," the dimpled spot from which the plant and roots grow. Each piece needs 30–45 cm of space around it.

Growing

Potatoes prefer **full sun** but tolerate some shade. The soil should be **fertile, humus rich, acidic, moist** and **well drained**, though potatoes adapt to most growing conditions and tolerate both hot and cold weather. Mound soil up around the plants to keep the tubers out of the light as they develop.

'Chieftan'

Harvesting

The tubers begin to form around the same time the plants begin to flower, usually sometime in August. From this point on, you can dig up a few tubers at a time as often as you need them.

The remaining crop should be dug up in fall once the plants have withered, but before the first hard frost. Let them dry for a few hours on the soil, then brush the dirt off and store the tubers in a cold, dark place. You can even save a few of the smaller tubers for planting the following spring.

Is your potato high or low in starch? To find out, cut one in half, rub the cut surfaces together and then try putting them back together. If they stick, the starch content is high. High-starch varieties are best for baking and mashing. Low-starch spuds are best for boiling and for potato salad.

Tips

These large, bushy plants with tiny, exotic-looking flowers are good filler plants for an immature border and are excellent at breaking up the soil in newer gardens.

Potatoes can easily be grown in containers, as long as there is adequate depth both for

the tubers to grow and to allow for mounding the soil up as the tubers mature. There are several containers on the market specifically for potatoes. Collapsible containers are perfect for gardeners with limited space, folding away for winter storage; some even come with a handy pocket for harvesting. You can also make your own potato container out of a 5-gallon bucket, or even up to a 32-gallon plastic garbage can; drill holes in the bottom for drainage.

Potatoes can also be grown in pots indoors, with the advantage that you won't have to worry about potato beetles. Use fingerling varieties, and plan for about 4 months of growing time.

Recommended

S. tuberosum is a bushy, mound-forming plant. It bears, white, pink or light purple flowers in late summer. The tubers can have rough or smooth, white, yellow, brown, red or blue skin and white, yellow, purple or blue flesh. A few popular varieties include '**All-Blue**,' with smooth, blue skin and light purple-blue flesh; '**Irish Cobbler**,' an heirloom with smooth, brown skin and white flesh that is widely adapted

'Kennebec'

to extreme temperatures; **'Norland,'** with smooth, red skin and white flesh; and **'Yukon Gold,'** with smooth, light beige skin and yellow flesh.

Some lesser known but worthwhile varieties include **'Kennebec,'** with its high yield of oblong tubers and its disease and drought tolerance; **'Chieftan,'** with round, red-skinned potatoes that are resistant to scab and other diseases; and **'Tolaas,'** a mid-season producer bearing large, smooth, white-fleshed potatoes with translucent skin. This one was bred for its adaptability to heavy and dry soils, and it stores for long periods once harvested.

'Banana' is a fingerling type with yellow skin and flesh. Its vigorous growth results in heavy yields. **'Austrian Crescent'** is another fingerling variety, with tan skin and yellow flesh. **'Purple Peruvian'** is also a fingerling, but it is purple inside and out.

Problems and Pests
Potatoes are susceptible to a variety of diseases, including scab. Avoid planting them in the same spot 2 years in a row. Potato beetle is the most troublesome insect pest.

All parts of the potato plant are **poisonous** *except the tubers, and they can become poisonous if they are exposed to light. Green flesh is an indication that your potatoes have been exposed to light.*

Radish

Raphanus

Features: rosette-forming annual; fast growing; edible roots
Height: 15–20 cm **Spread:** 10–15 cm

Radishes are grouped into two categories. Spring or salad radishes include the familiar round, red radishes and icicle radishes. Winter radishes, which include Oriental or daikon radishes and Spanish radishes, are eaten raw or cooked and can be pickled. Radishes are a great spicy addition to a variety of recipes far beyond the standard salad, so expand your culinary horizons and give them a try.

Starting

Direct sow seeds in spring, as soon as the soil warms up a bit and can be worked. Plants tolerate light frost. Successive, smaller plantings every 2 weeks will ensure a steady supply of radishes. Start daikon and other winter radishes in midsummer to be harvested in fall.

Growing

Radishes grow well in **full sun** or **light shade**. The soil should be of **average fertility, loose, humus rich, moist** and **well drained**. Heavy or rocky soils cause the roots to be rough, woody and unpleasant tasting.

Harvesting

Spring radishes should be picked and eaten as soon as the roots develop; some varieties are ready to harvest within a month. The flavour and texture deteriorate quickly if they are left in the ground or stored for too long.

Winter radishes started in midsummer will be ready for harvest in late fall. Store them in moist sand in a cool, dry location. They can also be pickled.

The greens of most radishes can be eaten just like beet tops or turnip tops. They are tasty fresh or steamed and are full of nutrients.

Tips

Their leafy, low-growing habit makes radishes good edging plants for borders, and they are excellent additions to container plantings both indoors and out. Use radishes for a quick-growing spring display that will be replaced by other plants once the weather warms up.

Radishes are also great nurse plants. If planted with mature plants or those that are small-seeded or slow to germinate, such as parsnips and carrots, radishes will shade out weeds and reduce evaporation.

Recommended

R. sativus forms a low clump of leaves. The edible roots can be long and slender or short and round; the skin can be red, purple, green, white or black; the taste ranges from mild to spicy hot. '**Cherry Belle**' is an extra-early variety with short tops and bright red skin. '**French Breakfast**' is a large, oblong, scarlet radish with white tips. '**Green Luobo**' is green inside and out. '**White Icicle**' bears long, slender, white roots from tip to stem. '**Black Spanish Round**' produces round roots 7–10 cm or larger, with crisp, white, spicy flesh and black skin. It is an excellent keeper.

R. sativus var. *longipinnatus* (daikon) varieties tend to be more mild in flavour than black types, and larger in size than red and white types. '**New Crown**' grows 30–35 cm long and 5 cm wide, with white skin and pale green tops. '**Omny**' grows 40 cm long. It is slow to bolt and likes cool temperatures.

Problems and Pests

Flea beetles and cabbage maggots are common problems for radishes.

Radishes tend to bolt in hot weather, causing the roots to develop an unpleasantly hot flavour. Choose icicle types for your summer growing because they are more tolerant of hot weather than the round, red varieties.

Rutabaga

Brassica

Features: rosette-forming biennial grown as an annual; blue-green foliage; edible roots
Height: 30–60 cm **Spread:** 10–20 cm

Rutabagas are often confused with or are used interchangeably with turnips. The two vegetables are closely related; they have a similar look, and both of them have a sweet, buttery, nutty flavour for soups, stews or just on their own as a side dish to any meal. The difference is that rutabagas are slightly larger, with a longer growing season; they also have better storage capability.

Starting

Young plants can be purchased at your local garden centre and planted after last frost, or you can sow seeds directly into the garden in spring. Give rutabagas up to 25 cm of space. Keep the seedbed moist until the plants germinate.

Growing

Rutabagas prefer to grow in **full sun**. The soil should be **fertile, moist** and **well drained**. The roots can develop discoloured centres in boron-deficient soil. Work agricultural boron into the soil if needed.

Harvesting

Rutabagas can be used as soon as they are plump and round, but they can also be left in the ground so the first few fall frosts sweeten the roots. Dig them up, cut the greens off and let them dry just enough that the dirt can be brushed off, then store them in moist sand in a cold, frost-free location for winter.

Tips

Rutabagas produce large, bushy clumps of blue-green foliage and can be included in the middle of a border where, though they aren't particularly showy, they provide an attractive, contrasting background for other plants.

Recommended

B. napus (rutabaga, swede, winter turnip) forms a large clump of smooth, waxy, blue-green leaves. The roots are most often white with purple tops, and most have yellow flesh, but white-fleshed varieties are available. '**American Purple Top**' is a common variety with sweet, fine-grained, yellow flesh that turns bright orange when cooked. '**Laurentian**' and its many variations are commonly available and are popular because they store well. Choose a variety that is clubroot resistant, if this disease is common in your region. '**Wilhelmsburger**' ('German Green Top') is a vigorous, disease-resistant heirloom variety with golden flesh and green shoulders. '**York**' is good for storing and is clubroot resistant.

Problems and Pests

Cabbage root maggots, cabbage worms, cabbage white butterfly larvae, aphids, flea beetles, rust, downy mildew, powdery mildew and clubroot are possible problems. Avoid planting any Brassica in the same spot in successive years.

The rutabaga originated in Europe and has been in cultivation for over 4000 years.

Sunchoke

Jerusalem Artichoke

Helianthus

Features: tall, bushy perennial; yellow flowers; edible tubers
Height: 1.8–3 m **Spread:** 60 cm–1.2 m

Sunchokes, of the sunflower family, are a native species that develop edible tubers, which taste like artichokes, radishes or water chestnuts, depending on who is describing the flavour. Known as "sun roots" prior to European settlers' arrival, these tubers were a diet staple for First Nations, and later for Europeans as well. The other common name, Jerusalem artichoke, is thought to have derived from the idea that the sunchokes were food for the "new Jerusalem."

Starting

Sunchokes can be sown directly into the garden, 30–90 cm apart depending on how much space is available, in spring around the last frost date. Water well until the plants become established. Sunchokes are perennial and will grow back each year as long as you leave some of the tubers in place in fall.

Growing

Sunchokes grow best in **full sun**. The soil should be of **average fertility, humus rich, moist** and **well drained**, though plants adapt to a variety of conditions. They become quite drought tolerant as summer progresses.

Harvesting

Sunchoke tubers are usually ready to harvest around the time of the first frost in fall. They should be stored in a cool, dry, well-ventilated area. They have only a small trace of starch but contain plenty of inulin, which turns into fructose when they're stored in a cold room, refrigerator or left in the ground. In fact, once the tubers are cooled in storage, they develop a much sweeter taste.

Tips

Sunchokes are striking at the back of a border and along fences and walls. These tall plants may need staking in windy locations.

Recommended

H. tuberosus is a tall, bushy, tuberous perennial. Bright yellow flowers are produced in late summer and fall. There are a great many sunchokes to choose from. '**Mulles Rose**' produces large, white tubers with rose-purple eyes. '**Stampede**' is an early yielding, large, white-fleshed sunchoke, ready in 90 days. '**Boston Red**' has large, rosy red tubers with smooth outer skin. '**Dwarf Sunray**' bears tender, crisp tubers that do not require peeling. '**Fuseau**' has a long, straight tuber, knob-free with white flesh. '**Jack's Copperclad**' is an heirloom variety and is difficult to find, but well worth the search. It bears plump, knobby tubers with dark copper or rose-purple skin and sweet flesh.

Problems and Pests

Sunchokes are generally problem free.

Sunchokes are crunchier and sweeter than potatoes, with a hint of artichoke. They can be boiled, baked, fried, steamed, stewed or eaten raw. They cook more quickly than potatoes do and become mushy if overcooked.

Turnip

Brassica

Features: clumping biennial grown as an annual; edible foliage; edible root
Height: 25–45 cm **Spread:** 15–20 cm

How this vegetable ended up with the likes of broccoli, Brussels sprouts and spinach as the most disliked veggies on any child's plate is difficult to figure out. I suspect that the cooking methods are to blame, as they all tended to be cooked until they were mush. Turnips have a sweet, buttery, nutty flavour for soups, stews or just on their own as a side dish to any meal. Just be careful not to overcook them.

Starting

Young plants can be purchased and planted after the last frost, or you can sow seeds directly into the garden in spring. Plant turnips 15–20 cm apart. Keep the seedbed moist until the plants germinate. Several small, successive sowings will provide you with turnips for longer.

Growing

Turnips prefer to grow in **full sun**. The soil should be **fertile, moist** and **well drained**. The roots can develop discoloured centres in boron-deficient soil. Work agricultural boron into the soil if needed. Don't let the plants dry out for long periods, as this will adversely affect the quality of not only the roots but the leaves as well.

Harvesting

The leaves can be harvested a few at a time from each plant as needed. They are best fresh when young and tender. They can be eaten when more mature as well but should be cooked.

The roots should be harvested as soon as they are plump and round. Dig them up, cut the greens off and let them dry just enough that the dirt can be brushed off, then use them as soon as possible. Turnips do not keep well when stored.

Tips
Turnips produce large, bushy clumps of foliage and can be included in the middle of a border where, though they aren't particularly showy, they provide an attractive, contrasting background for flowering plants. Small turnip varieties are also suitable for containers, even window boxes if you want easy access to the greens.

Recommended
B. rapa (turnip, summer turnip) produces large clumps of edible foliage. The root, or swelling, grows at the surface of the soil with the top third exposed above ground level. This top is often purple-skinned, while the bottom two-thirds is white. The flesh is usually white or yellowish white. **'Purple Top White Globe'** and **'White Lady'** are popular cultivars. **'Just Right'** is ready in 70 days, producing rounded, mild-flavoured white roots, inside and out. **'Hinona Kabu'** is an unusual turnip, with a large, elongated root. Both the greens and the root are delicious. **'Milan'** is a baby turnip with a buttery flavour, bright red shoulders and white bottoms. **'Oasis'** can be picked at any size. The super-sweet roots can be eaten raw, whole like an apple or grated for salads and snacks. The flavour has been compared to that of a melon.

Problems and Pests
Cabbage root maggots, cabbage worms, cabbage white butterfly larvae, aphids, flea beetles, rust, downy mildew, powdery mildew and clubroot are possible problems. Avoid planting any Brassica in the same spot in successive years.

Some turnip varieties are grown for nothing but their edible greens.

Asparagus

Asparagus

Features: ferny perennial; edible spring shoots; small, white, summer flowers; red berries
Height: 60 cm–1.5 m **Spread:** 60 cm–1.2 m

The large, ferny growth that asparagus develops comes as quite a surprise to first-time growers who may only have seen tidy bunches of spears at the grocery store. Asparagus is a member of the lily family, and well-established plants can last a lifetime, producing tasty spears every spring.

Starting

Most people begin with 1-year-old crowns, or roots, purchased from a garden centre. Plant roots into a well-prepared area. Work plenty of compost into the bed, then dig a trench or hole about 45 cm deep. Lay the roots 45–60 cm apart from each other or other plants. Cover the roots with 5–10 cm of soil and, as they sprout up, gradually cover them with more soil until the trench or hole is filled. Water and mulch well.

Growing

Asparagus grows well in **full sun** or **partial shade** with protection from the hot afternoon sun. The soil should be **fertile, humus rich, moist** and **well drained**. Apply a 10 cm layer of compost in spring and late summer. Weed regularly; asparagus is most productive if it doesn't have a lot of competition from other plants.

'Guelph Millennium'

'Jersey Knight' produces premium quality spears up to 2 cm thick. 'Jersey Supreme' is known for its sheer abundance of spears produced once established, up to 4.5 kg per season. 'Martha Washington' and 'Mary Washington' are traditional, productive strains. 'Purple Passion' produces sweet and tender spears, but there is a slightly lesser yield with this cultivar because it is not often predominantly male. The purple spears turn green when cooked. 'Viking' is one of the hardiest varieties available.

Problems and Pests

Rust can be a problem, so choose resistant cultivars.

Asparagus is dioecious—male and female flowers are borne on separate plants. Male plants are reputed to produce the greatest number of spears.

'Purple Passion'

Harvesting

Asparagus spears started from roots are ready to be harvested 2 years after planting. Snap or cut the spears off at ground level for up to about 4 weeks in spring and early summer. When new spears are thinner than a pencil, you should stop harvesting and let the plants grow in.

Tips

This hardy perennial is a welcome treat in spring and a beautiful addition to the back of a border. It can also be used as a screen or divider.

Recommended

A. officinalis forms an airy mound of ferny growth. Small, white, summer flowers are followed by bright red berries. 'Jersey Giant' is known for its high yield and production of the largest spears, while

Broccoli

Brassica

Features: bushy, upright annual; blue-green foliage; dense clusters of edible flowers
Height: 30–90 cm **Spread:** 30–45 cm

Although usually thought of as a vegetable, broccoli could more accurately be called an edible flower. It is the large, dense flower clusters that are generally eaten, though the stems and leaves are also edible. If you plan to freeze some florets, you may prefer a large-headed selection. If you want to enjoy the broccoli for longer without storing any, you may prefer the small-headed varieties that produce plenty of side shoots.

Starting

Broccoli can be started from seed indoors or planted directly into the garden. Sow seeds indoors 4–6 weeks before the last frost date, and plant seedlings out or direct sow into the garden around the last frost date, usually 30 cm apart.

Growing

Broccoli prefers **full sun**. The soil should be **fertile, moist** and **well drained**. Broccoli performs best in cooler weather. Mix compost into the soil, and add a layer of mulch to keep the soil moist. Don't let broccoli dry out excessively or it will delay flowering.

Harvesting

Broccoli forms a central head, and some varieties also produce side shoots. Cut the heads cleanly from the plant with a sharp knife. If you leave them too long on the plant, the bright yellow flowers will open.

Tips

Broccoli, with its blue-green foliage, is an interesting accent plant. Tuck small groups of it into your borders and mixed

'Broccolo Verde Romanesco'

beds for a striking contrast. This plant is susceptible to quite a few pests, and spacing it out in small groups rather than planting it in rows helps reduce the severity of potential problems.

Broccoli will also do well in a container as long as it has enough room to grow.

Recommended

B. oleracea var. *botrytis* is an upright plant with a stout, leafy central stem. Flowers form at the top of the plant and sometimes on side shoots that emerge from just above each leaf. Maturity dates vary from 45 to 100 days. '**Belstar**' produces domed, small-beaded, deep green heads. '**Gypsy**' produces a large central head and is one of the most heat-tolerant cultivars. '**Martha**' is an early variety, short and compact and very heat tolerant. It bears large heads with small beads. '**Nutri-Bud**,' '**Packman**' and '**Premium Crop**' are early-maturing cultivars that produce lots of side shoots after the main head is cut.

Broccoli is also available in novelty selections. '**Broccoli Mini Hybrid Apollo**' (asparagus broccoli) has the appearance of headless broccoli. The main floret is harvested first, followed by the abundant side shoots. '**Broccolo Verde Romanesco**'

(broccoflower) resembles a cross between cauliflower and broccoli. Its texture is similar to both, but it tastes more like broccoli.

Problems and Pests

Problems with cutworms, leaf miners, caterpillars, root maggots, cabbage white butterflies, white rust, downy mildew and powdery mildew can occur. Avoid planting any Brassica in the same spot in successive years.

Cabbage white butterfly larvae are tough to spot in a head of broccoli. Break heads into pieces and soak them in salted water for 10 minutes. Doing so kills the larvae and causes them to float to the surface.

Brussels Sprout

Brassica

Features: bushy, upright annual; blue-green foliage; edible buds along the stem
Height: up to 60 cm **Spread:** up to 45 cm

Brussels sprouts are nutrient rich and fibre packed, and they deserve a more prominent place on our plates. Love them or hate them, Brussels sprouts are at the very least a garden curiosity. The sprouts form on the stout central stem at the base of each leaf. By fall, the display is unique and eye-catching.

Starting

Brussels sprouts can be purchased as small transplants in spring, or seeds can be started indoors about 6 weeks before you expect to transplant the seedlings into the garden. Sowing the seeds into peat pots or pellets makes transplanting easy. Space the seedlings 30–45 cm apart, depending on the variety; check the seed packet or plant tag.

Growing

Brussels sprouts grow well in **full sun**. The soil should be **fertile, moist** and **well drained**. Brussels sprouts need a fairly long growing season to produce sprouts of any appreciable size, so they should be planted out as early as possible. Regular moisture encourages them to mature

quickly. Once you see sprouts starting to form, you may wish to remove some of the stem leaves to give the sprouts more room to grow.

Harvesting

Pick sprouts as soon as they are large and plump, but before they begin to open. A light frost can improve the flavour of the sprouts. The entire plant can be pulled up, and if you remove the roots, leaves and top of the plant, the sprouts can be stored on the stem in a cool place for up to 4 weeks. Be sure to keep an eye on them because they can go bad quickly. They can also be frozen for later use.

Tips

Brussels sprouts can provide a leafy backdrop for your flowering annuals and perennials all summer; then, just as the garden is fading, they create an interesting focal point as the plump little sprouts develop.

Recommended

B. oleracea var. *gemnifera* is an upright plant that develops a single leafy stem. Sprouts form at the base of each leaf along the stem. The leaves are blue-green, often

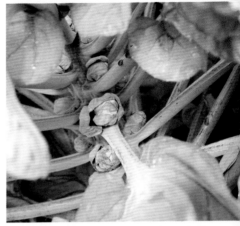

with white mid-ribs and stems. '**Bitesize**' is a sweet selection that produces well-spaced sprouts that are easy to harvest. They remain firm on the stem for a long period of time compared to other varieties. '**Catskill**' produces abundant sprouts with a cabbage flavour. They're very tender and small, reaching only 2–5 cm across, on very strong stalks. '**Trafalgar**' produces a heavy crop of super sweet, medium-sized sprouts that keep for a long period on the stalk. '**Bedford Fillbasket**,' '**Jade Cross**' and '**Vancouver**' are also popular cultivars.

Problems and Pests

Problems with cutworms, leaf miners, caterpillars, root maggots, aphids, cabbage white butterfly larvae, white rust, downy mildew and powdery mildew can occur. Avoid planting any Brassica in the same spot in successive years.

When picked after a light frost, steamed and served with butter, Brussels sprouts are delicious. To avoid overcooking them, cut an X about one-quarter of the way through the stem end of each sprout to help the inside cook at the same rate as the outside. You can also roast them in the oven with olive oil and garlic to bring out their sweetness.

Cabbage

Brassica

Features: rosette-forming biennial grown as an annual; loose or dense, round or upright, smooth or crinkled, green, red or purple, edible foliage **Height:** 45–60 cm **Spread:** 30–45 cm

Cabbages of every size, shape and texture are easy to grow, and they create a dense, leafy, often colourful display. They come in three forms: green with smooth leaves, green with crinkled leaves and red or purple, usually with smooth leaves.

Starting

Start seeds indoors about 4–6 weeks before you plan to transplant the seedlings outdoors. You can also direct sow cabbage into the garden around the last frost date as long as the soil has warmed up a bit. Early selections can be planted up to 30 cm apart, while late selections should be planted up to 45 cm apart. If you find average cabbages too large, plant them closer together to get smaller, tighter heads.

Growing

Cabbages grow best in **full sun**. The soil should be **fertile, moist** and **well drained**. They prefer cool growing conditions and benefit from mulch to retain moisture during hot weather.

Harvesting

The leaves of young cabbage plants can be eaten. When a good-sized head has developed, cut it cleanly from the plant. Smaller heads often develop once the main head has been cut.

Cabbages are frost hardy, and the last of them can be left in the ground through fall, then stored in a cold, frost-free location. Cabbages that take a long time to mature generally store better than quick-maturing types.

Tips

Grow several varieties of cabbages because the different colours, textures and maturing times will create an interesting display, whether in rows or mixed into your borders.

Recommended

B. oleracea var. *capitata* is a low, leafy rosette that develops a dense head over summer. Leaves may be green, blue-green, red or purple and smooth or crinkled. It matures in 60–140 days, depending on the variety.

Some popular smooth-leaved, green varieties are **'January King,' 'Bartolo,' 'Early Jersey Wakefield,' 'Lennox'** and **'Parel.'** **'Blue Vantage'** is a mid-season selection, producing large, dense, short-cored, blue-green heads. It is best eaten fresh. **'Danish Ballhead'** is a later variety with large, light green heads. **'Caraflex'** is interesting because it is pointed like a teardrop. It is

incredibly sweet and is also one of the most tender cabbages to grow in Canada. It's ready 50 days after transplanting.

Popular crinkled or savoy types include **'Savoy Blue,' 'Savoy King,' 'Taler'** and **'Wirosa.'** Popular red cabbages include **'Buscaro,' 'Red Acre Early,' 'Red Drumhead,' 'Red Express'** and **'Ruby Dynasty.'**

Problems and Pests

Problems with cutworms, leaf miners, caterpillars, root maggots, aphids, cabbage white butterfly larvae, white rust, downy mildew and powdery mildew can occur. Avoid planting any Brassica in the same spot in successive years.

To protect cabbage from egg-laying moths, make a plastic butterfly screen. Simply hammer stakes into the ground at each corner of the row or patch of cabbage. Cut out simple, quarter-sized moths or butterflies from a white plastic container lid and thread them onto fishing line. Attach the ends of the line to the stakes, creating a grid pattern. Cabbage butterflies will think this territory has already been taken and is off limits.

'Copenhagen'

Cauliflower

Brassica

Features: bushy, upright annual; white, purple, green, yellow or orange, edible flower heads
Height: 45–60 cm **Spread:** 30–45 cm

Maybe it's not everyone's favourite, but with the interesting assortment of colours now available, cauliflower can create quite an interesting display in the late-summer or fall garden, not to mention how tasty it can be. Tuck a few plants here and there in your mixed borders to shake things up a bit and to increase your harvest.

Starting

Cauliflower can be sown directly into the garden around the last frost date, or you can start it indoors about 4 weeks before you plan to set it outdoors. Standard-sized heads should be spaced 30–45 cm apart; smaller selections can be planted closer together.

Growing

Cauliflower grows best in **full sun**. The soil should be **fertile, moist** and **well drained**. This plant doesn't like persistently hot weather (more than 2 weeks with temperatures over 27° C), but it's rarely a problem, even in comparatively hot gardens. Cauliflower must have a rich soil that stays evenly moist, or heads may form poorly, if at all. Mix plenty of compost into the soil, and then mulch with compost to help keep the soil moist.

mature in as few as 45 days. Popular white-headed cultivars include '**Early Dawn**,' '**Snowball**' and '**Symphony**.' '**Graffiti**' and '**Violet Queen**' are purple-headed cultivars; they generally turn green when cooked. '**Cheddar**' and '**Orange Bouquet**' are orange-headed cultivars. Green-headed cultivars include '**Green Harmony**' and '**Veronica**,' whose florets form pointed, tapering peaks.

Problems and Pests

Problems with cutworms, leaf miners, caterpillars, root maggots, aphids, cabbage white butterfly larvae, white rust, downy mildew and powdery mildew can occur. Avoid planting any Brassica in the same spot in successive years.

Cauliflower was once touted as a difficult vegetable to grow, but it is now considered to be quite easy to grow and is highly regarded by most gardeners.

Harvesting

Unlike broccoli, cauliflower does not develop secondary heads once the main one is cut. Cut the head cleanly from the plant when it is mature. You can then compost the plant.

Tips

White cauliflower may turn yellow or greenish unless some of the leaves are tied over the head to shade it from the sun. Tie some of the outer leaves together over the head with elastic or string when you first notice the head forming.

Unlike white cauliflower, the purple-, green-, yellow- or orange-headed varieties need no shading while they develop. The coloured selections are pretty in mixed ornamental gardens.

Recommended

B. oleracea var. *botrytis* is leafy and upright with dense, edible flower clusters in the centre of the plant. Most selections take 70–85 days to mature, though some

Celery

Apium

Features: upright biennial grown as an annual; bright green, edible leaves and stems
Height: 45 cm **Spread:** 25 cm

Tender, ribbed stalks of celery fresh from the garden are quite different than store-bought celery. The flavour of unblanched stems is much stronger but much appreciated by many gardeners, and the wide variety of uses for this veggie far surpasses the ever-faithful CheezWhiz or peanut butter spread on top.

Starting

Celery seed should be started indoors at least 8 weeks and up to 12 weeks before you plan to transplant it outdoors. Be patient; seed can take up to 3 weeks to germinate. Be sure to keep the planting medium moist, but not soggy. Plant out once the last frost date has passed and the soil has warmed up.

Growing

Celery grows best in **full sun** but enjoys light or afternoon shade in hot weather. The soil should be **fertile, humus rich, moist** and **well drained**. Allowing the soil to dry out too much will give you a poor quality, bad-tasting vegetable. Mulch plants to conserve moisture.

In late summer, you can mound soil around the celery stalks, wrap them in newspaper or surround the base of each

XP 266,' 'Conquistador,' 'Golden Self-Blanching,' 'Red Stalk' and 'Utah 52-70' are popular cultivars. **'Victoria'** is an earlier variety, with strong stalks, high resistance to bolting and a crisp texture. **'Tango'** is ready in 80 days, producing stronger flavour than most. The stalks are tender, with less fibre, and the plant overall is more tolerant to excessive heat and moisture stress.

Problems and Pests
Problems with fungal blight, mosaic virus, fusarium yellows, bacterial and fungal rot, leaf spot and caterpillars can occur.

Cold nights can cause celery to flower, leaving the stalks inedible, or at least unpalatable.

plant with a milk carton with the top and bottom cut out to shade the stems from the sun, which will encourage the development of the pale green or blanched stems we are familiar with. Unblanched stalks have a stronger flavour that some people prefer.

Harvesting
Celery stalks can be harvested 1–2 at a time from each plant for most of summer. If you are blanching the stems before picking them, they will be ready for harvesting 2–3 weeks after the stalks are covered. A light touch of frost can sweeten the flavour of celery.

Tips
Celery has light green leaves that create a very bushy backdrop for flowering plants with less attractive, spindly growth. It does well in containers as long as it's kept well watered and the pot is at least 20 cm deep.

Recommended
A. graveolens var. *dulce* is a bushy, upright plant with attractive, light to bright green foliage. It matures in 80–120 days. 'Celery

Fiddlehead Fern

Matteuccia

Features: perennial fern; attractive foliage; edible, tender shoots
Height: 90 cm–1.5 m **Spread:** 30–90 cm

These popular, classic ferns are revered for their delicious, emerging spring fronds and their stately, vase-shaped habit. The fiddleheads—the tightly coiled, new spring fronds—are only available for a few weeks in an entire year. They taste wonderful lightly steamed and served with butter. Remove the bitter, reddish brown, papery coating before steaming.

Starting

Crowns can be purchased and planted out in spring once the threat of frost has passed but are often available throughout the growing season, either as bareroot or potted stock. They are often sold as ornamental plants in the perennial department of your local garden centre.

This particular species of fern spreads by underground runners. Space the plants approximately 60–90 cm apart. New plants will develop from the main root and can be divided and moved or left in place.

Growing

Fiddlehead ferns prefer **light shade** or **partial shade** but tolerate full shade, or full sun if the soil stays moist. The soil should be **average to fertile, humus rich, neutral to acidic** and **moist**. Add compost to the planting hole to achieve a slightly acidic soil.

Moisture for ferns is rather critical. If the area is prone to drying out, use thick mulch around the base of the plants, and

possibly a soaker hose buried under the mulch, on a timer, to keep the roots and soil consistently moist. Leaves may scorch if the soil is not moist enough.

Harvesting
Let plants become established for a couple of years before you begin harvesting. Pick new fronds in spring just as they are beginning to uncurl. Mature ostrich ferns produce an average of 7 fronds. When picking fiddleheads, make sure to pick no more than 3 (no more than half) per plant to allow enough surface area for the plant to thrive throughout the growing season.

Tips
These ferns are often found growing wild alongside woodland streams and creeks and appreciate a moist woodland garden. Fiddlehead ferns are also useful in shaded borders and are quick to spread.

Agriculture Canada determined that fiddleheads contain even more antioxidants than blueberries, are packed with omega-3 fatty acids and dietary fibre, are low in sodium and contain vitamins A and C, niacin, potassium, phosphorus, iron and magnesium.

Recommended
M. struthiopteris (*M. pensylvanica*; ostrich fern) forms a circular cluster of slightly arching, feathery fronds. Stiff, brown, fertile fronds, covered in reproductive spores, stick up in the centre of the cluster in late summer and persist through winter. They are popular in dried arrangements.

Problems and Pests
These ferns rarely have any problems.

*Fiddleheads should **not** be eaten fresh. They must be cooked first to remove the shikimic acid.*

Leek

Allium

Features: edible, upright perennial often grown as an annual; long, arching, blue-green foliage
Height: 30–90 cm **Spread:** 10–20 cm

Leeks can rival most ornamental grasses for garden presence. The plants are strongly upright with stunning dark blue-green leaves that arch from the main stem. Planted in a small group, they are a welcome addition to any border.

Starting

Leeks can be sown directly in the garden, but because they take quite a long time to mature, you may want to start them indoors 8–10 weeks before you plan to plant them outdoors. Once the stems reach the diameter of a pencil, transplant them to the garden, roughly 10–15 cm apart, in a trench 10 cm deep. Or, you can purchase started plants when you are ready to plant them outdoors.

Growing

Leeks grow best in **full sun**. The soil should be **fertile** and **well drained**, but plants adapt to most well-drained soils. Improve soil by mixing in compost or adding a layer of compost mulch once you have planted. Mound mulch or soil up around the base of the plants as summer progresses to encourage tender, white growth low on the plant.

If you don't harvest all your leeks, they can be left to flower and go to seed. They will

Recommended

A. ampeloprasum **subsp.** *porrum* is an upright perennial with blue-green leaves that cascade from the central stem. Globe-shaped clusters of flowers are borne the second year from planting. Many varieties are available. **'King Richard'** produces large leeks with white stems in only 75 days. This variety is not hardy enough for overwintering but can withstand a medium to heavy frost without losing its texture or flavour. **'Lancelot'** is ready in 90 days, producing bluish, erect foliage with bright white stalks. This selection can be sown tightly together, without thinning, for a summer harvest of smaller, tender baby leeks. **'Monstrous Carentan'** is a hardy, vigorous leek that is sweet, mild and very cold tolerant. It is ready in roughly 110 days.

Problems and Pests

Problems with rot, mildew, smut, rust, leaf spot, onion flies and thrips can occur.

Leeks were once a popular cure for venomous bites, ulcers, nosebleeds, poor eyesight, drunkenness, toothaches, coughs, headaches and many other ills.

return year after year, and new seedlings can be allowed to grow in to replace fading plants.

Harvesting

Leeks can be harvested as soon as they are mature in early fall, but because they are so hardy, you can just harvest them as you need them until the ground begins to freeze. At that point you should pull up any you want for winter use.

Leeks keep for several weeks in the refrigerator if you cut the roots short and wrap the leeks in plastic. For longer storage, leeks can be frozen. Be sure to double bag them so the onion-like flavour doesn't seep into any other food you have in the freezer.

Tips

Leeks, with their bright blue-green leaves, are one of the most ornamental of all the onions. Plant them in groups in your beds and borders, or in a container as long as it is deep enough.

Oriental Cabbage

Brassica

Features: upright annual; edible, attractive foliage
Height: 45 cm **Spread:** 30 cm

A classic Asian vegetable, Oriental cabbage is an interesting addition to the garden and a tasty ingredient in stir-fries and soups. It has light or dark green, white-veined leaves with undulating edges.

Starting

Start seeds indoors about 4–6 weeks before you plan to transplant the seedlings outdoors. You can also direct sow Oriental cabbage into the garden after the last frost date when the soil has warmed up a bit.

Growing

Oriental cabbage grows best in **full sun**. The soil should be **fertile, moist** and **well drained**. It prefers cool growing conditions and benefits from mulch to retain moisture during hot weather, but it is more tolerant of warm, humid weather than some of the other members of the Brassica family, making it a useful addition to Canadian gardens where the temperature tends to be hotter.

Harvesting

Oriental cabbage comes in two basic forms: solid heads that are cut whole, and looser heads with leaves that can be removed as needed.

Tips

Oriental cabbage can be grown in containers, where it can be combined with

other edible or flowering plants. Dotted through a border, it creates a low but upright feature, adding its unique colour and form.

Recommended

B. rapa* subsp. *chinensis (pac choi, bok choi) forms a loose clump of blue-green leaves with thick, fleshy, white or light green stems. There are three types: green stem, white stem and specialty. **'Hanakan'** is a compact Japanese green stem hybrid that is ready to harvest in 45 days. **'Dwarf Pak Choi'** (baby bok choi) is a white-stemmed variety that is mild in flavour. Harvest when it is 10 cm tall. **'Golden Yellow'** is a specialty hybrid that bears yellowish green leaves from root to tip. **'Red Violet Tatsoi'** is a deep purple variety.

B. rapa* subsp. *pekinensis (Chinese cabbage, nappa cabbage) forms a dense head of tightly packed leaves. There are four types: barrel head, loose head, fluffy top and Michihili. **'Optiko'** has a barrel shape with prominent white veins and ribs. It matures faster than most others and is

mild tasting with a crisp texture. **'Vitaminna,'** a loose head type, has dark green leaves, white stems, is slow to bolt and has a high concentration of vitamin A. **'Kaisin Hakusai'** is a fluffy top cabbage with frilly outer leaves that become more blanched toward the centre. **'Green Rocket,'** a Michihili type, resembles an endive or chicory head, but jumbo sized. It is grown for its sweetness. The tight heads are more mild and tender than western cabbages.

Problems and Pests

Problems with cutworms, leaf miners, caterpillars, root maggots, aphids, cabbage white butterfly larvae, white rust, downy mildew and powdery mildew can occur. Avoid planting any Brassica in the same spot in successive years.

Many seed catalogues offer a selection of Oriental vegetables. Some of them are recognizable cultivars or species of plants, while others are unique. Try a few to expand your vegetable repertoire.

Bean

Phaseolus

Features: bushy or twining annual; red, white or bicoloured flowers; edible pods or seeds
Height: 30 cm–2.4 m **Spread:** 30–45 cm

This incredibly diverse group of legumes is sure to please everyone; there are few things as delicious as fresh beans for dinner, straight out of the garden. Most people are familiar with the string bean, but there is so much more to this group of vegetables. The selection is almost endless.

Starting

Beans are quite possibly one of the easiest plants to grow from seed. The seeds are large and easy to handle, and they sprout quickly in warm, moist soil; they will sprout even quicker if you soak them in water overnight. Plant the seeds directly in the garden after the last frost date has passed and the soil has warmed up. They can be planted 10–20 cm apart.

Growing

Beans grow best in **full sun**, but they tolerate some light afternoon shade. The soil should be of **average fertility** and **well drained**. Bush beans are self-supporting, but climbing beans need a pole or trellis to grow up. The support structure should be in place at planting time to avoid disturbing the young plants or damaging their roots.

Harvesting

Various types of beans should be picked at different stages in their development. Green, runner, wax or snap beans are picked once the pod is a good size but still young and tender. Beans that are eaten as immature seeds should be picked when the pods are full and the seeds are fleshy and moist.

Legumes (including beans) are known for being able to fix nitrogen from the air into the soil through a symbiotic relationship with bacteria, which attach to the roots as small nodules. The bacteria, present in most soils, turn the nitrogen from the air into useable nitrogen for the plant; in return, the plant feeds and supports the bacteria.

Recommended

P. coccineus (runner bean) is a vigorous climbing plant with red or sometimes white or bicoloured flowers. **'Scarlet Runner'** has bright red flowers and is one of the best and best-known cultivars. The beans can be eaten with the pod when they are young and tender, or the plants can be left to mature and the pink and purple spotted beans can be dried. Plants produce

'Scarlett Runner'

Beans for drying are left to mature on the plant. Once the plant begins to die back and before the seedpods open, cut the entire plant off at ground level, leaving the nitrogen-fixing roots to enrich the soil, and hang it upside down indoors to finish drying; then remove the beans from the pods and store them in airtight containers in a cool, dry place. The beans will keep for 10–12 months.

Tips

Beans are ornamental, with attractive leaves and plentiful flowers. Climbing beans can be grown up fences, trellises, obelisks and poles to create a screen or feature planting. Bush beans can be used to make low, temporary hedges or can be planted in small groups in a border. All beans will do well in containers.

Bush beans can become less productive and look unattractive as summer wears on. Pull them up and plant something else in their place, or plant them with companions that mature more slowly to fill in the space left by the faded bean plants.

edible beans in 70 days but need about 100 days for dry beans.

P. lunatus (lima bean) may be climbing or bush, depending on the cultivar. The beans are eaten as immature seeds and should be picked when the pods are plump but the seeds are still tender. They take 70–85 days to mature. **'Fordhook'** is a popular bush variety, and **'King of the Garden'** is a good climbing selection.

P. vulgaris (wax bean, green bean, bush bean, snap bean, dry bean) is probably the largest group of beans and includes bush beans and pole beans. Some are eaten immature in the pod, and others are grown to maturity and used as dry beans. Bush bean cultivars may be yellow, such as **'Gold Rush'** and **'Sunburst'**; green, such as **'Ambra'** and **'Stallion'**; or purple-podded, such as **'Royal Burgundy.'** Purple beans turn bright green when cooked. Bush beans take 50–60 days to mature. **'Concador,'** a dwarf bush bean, is ideal for containers, producing 12 cm long, slender, pale yellow beans for a longer period than most other selections. **'Tema'** tolerates cool, wet soils. It produces for a longer

period than most and holds its flavour. Pole beans, such as **'Blue Lake'** and **'Kentucky Blue,'** take 50–55 days to mature. Dry beans are usually bush plants and take about 100 days to mature. They include kidney, pinto and navy beans. A popular selection for home growers is the red and white spotted **'Jacob's Cattle.'** Shell (or shelling) beans come in both pole and dwarf varieties and can produce big harvests in small gardens. Most beans can be used as shell beans, which have the pods removed before they are cooked or dried. **'Supremo'** is ready for harvest in 85 days.

Problems and Pests

Pick beans only when plants are dry to reduce the spread of disease. Problems with leaf spot, bacterial blight, rust, bean beetles and aphids can occur. Disease-infected plants should be destroyed, not composted, once you've harvested what you can.

Climbing beans are popular among gardeners with limited space because you can get more beans for less space.

Corn

Zea

Features: annual grass; broad, strap-shaped leaves; tassel-like flowers
Height: 1.2–1.8 m **Spread:** 30–60 cm

Widely grown by First Nations peoples in both North and South America, corn is one of the "three sisters" of Native gardens: corn, beans and squash. The three were grown together as companions. The beans fixed nitrogen in the soil and could climb up the corn for support. The large leaves of squash shaded the soil and kept weeds to a minimum.

Starting

Start seed directly in the garden once the last frost date has passed and the soil has warmed; seed will rot in cold soil. Corn takes 75–110 days to mature. If your growing season is short, you may prefer to start your corn 4–6 weeks early in peat pots and transplant it to the garden after the last frost date.

Growing

Corn grows best in **full sun**. The soil should be **fertile, moist** and **well drained**. As the plant develops, mound more soil around its base; the stem will develop roots in this soil, and the plant will be stronger and less likely to blow over in a strong wind.

Do not remove the tassels at the top of the plant. These male tassels shed pollen onto the silk of the female cob. Each silk thread is attached to a kernel. If no pollen falls onto the silk, no kernel will form. Shaking the plants when the pollen is being shed can help increase pollination.

Harvesting

Corn is ready to pick when the silks start to turn brown and the kernels are plump. Peel the husk back just slightly to check on the kernels.

Use heirloom varieties as quickly as possible after picking because they begin to turn starchy as soon as they are picked. Newer selections have been modified to increase their ability to stay sweet after picking, and can be stored for a while.

Tips

Corn is an architectural grass. Plant it in groups of 5–9 in your beds and borders. Also, because corn is wind pollinated, planting it in groups rather than rows improves pollination rates when you are growing only a few plants.

Recommended

Z. mays is a sturdy, upright grass with bright green leaves. **Var.** *rugosa* (sweet corn) matures in 65–80 days and falls into several categories that gauge both how sweet the corn is and how quickly the sugar turns to starch once the corn is picked. Some of the sweeter corns are less tolerant of cold soils. Kernels can be white or yellow, or cobs may have both colours. **Mirai Series** is a group of hybrids regarded as one of the most delicious corn series available. Sugar-enhanced selections are also very popular. **'Buttergold'** was bred for northern climates and produces all-yellow cobs with excellent flavour. **'Frisky'** has sugary, tender, creamy, bico-loured kernels. **'Early Sunglow'** is a nor-mal sugar corn, bearing extra-early, yellow cobs. It is ideal for cold-weather planting.

Problems and Pests

Corn earworms, aphids, caterpillars, downy mildew, rust, smut and fungal leaf spots can cause problems for corn.

To ensure maximum sweetness, cobs should be immersed in ice-cold water as soon as possible after picking, and left in the water until cooked. Also keep picked cobs out of the hot sun.

Cucumber

Cucumis

Features: trailing or climbing annual vine; yellow flowers; edible fruit
Height: 30 cm when trailing **Spread:** 1.2–2.4 m when trailing

'Alibi'

Cucumbers are popular fresh in salads and of course as pickles. One myth is that there are few ways to use this vegetable in our daily diet; however, if you browse through a vegetarian cookbook, you'll find that they're quite versatile in the culinary arts.

Starting

Cucumbers can be started indoors about 4 weeks before the last frost date or sown directly into the garden once the last frost date has passed and the soil has warmed up. If you are starting your plants indoors, plant the seeds in peat pots so the roots will not be damaged or disturbed when you transplant them outdoors.

Growing

Cucumbers grow well in **full sun** or **light shade**. The soil should be **fertile, moist** and **well drained**. Consistent moisture is most important when plants are germinating and once fruit is being produced.

If you are growing your cucumbers up a trellis or other support, you will probably need to tie the vines in place. Use soft ties to avoid damaging the plants.

Harvesting

Pickling cucumbers are picked while they are young and small. Slicing cucumbers can be picked when mature, or when small if you want to use them for pickling. Long, slender Oriental cucumbers are picked when mature and tend to be sweeter, developing no bitter flavour with age.

Tips

Cucumbers are versatile trailing plants. They can be left to wind their way through the other plants in your garden or grown up trellises or other supports.

The mound-forming varieties make attractive additions to container gardens. Try them with other salad plants such as tomatoes, green peppers and basil.

Recommended

C. sativus is a trailing annual vine with coarse leaves and bristly stems. It matures in 45–60 days. Popular slicing and salad cucumbers include the long, slender '**English Telegraph**' and '**Sweet Slender**'; All America Selections winner '**Fanfare**,' a prolific bush selection; and the high-yielding '**Stonewall**.' '**Armenian**' is a strong, vigorous heirloom cucumber with thin, light green skin. '**Burpless**' was bred for those who experience a bit of gassiness after eating cucumbers. This hybrid is mild and non-astringent, with a thin, tender skin. '**Straight Eight**' has superb flavour.

Novelty cucumber '**Tondo di Manduria**' produces rounded fruits about the size of a lemon, striped with dark and light green. If left to grow larger, the fruit can be treated like a melon. '**Lemon**' is a prolific heirloom variety, bearing oval, bright yellow fruits with a slight lemon flavour on vigorous vines. '**Long White**' has a thin, tender, white skin.

Popular pickling cultivars include the disease-tolerant, semi-bush '**Cross Country**' and the prolific, bushy '**Patio Pickles**.' '**Alibi**' is vigourous and versatile. The mature fruits can reach 7–10 cm long but are often harvested at 5 cm for smoother pickles.

Problems and Pests

Problems with powdery mildew, downy mildew, mosaic virus, white flies, aphids, cucumber beetles, bacterial wilt, leaf spot, scab and ring spot can occur.

Cucumbers keep producing fruit as long as you don't let the fruit stay on the vines for too long. Pick cucumbers as soon as they are a good size for eating. The more you pick, the more the plants will produce.

Pea

Pisum

Features: climbing annual; white flowers; edible pods and seeds (peas)
Height: 30 cm–1.5 m **Spread:** 10–20 cm

There is no replacement for picking peas straight from the vine on a summer's day in the garden and eating them straight from the pod. The flavour is far superior to any pea you can buy in the store—fresh is best.

Starting

Peas appreciate cool spring weather. They can be sown directly outdoors as soon as the soil has dried out a bit and can be worked, and they benefit from an overnight soaking in water before planting. The seeds can rot in cold, wet soil, but a light frost won't do them any harm.

Growing

Peas grow well in **full sun**. The soil should be **average to fertile, humus rich, moist** and **well drained**.

Peas can grow to a wide range of heights, but all benefit from a support of some kind to climb. They develop small tendrils that twine around twiggy branches, nets or chain-link fences. Make sure the support is in place before your seeds sprout because the shallow roots are easily damaged.

Harvesting

Pick peas when they are young and tender. Use both hands—one to hold the plant and one to pull the pod—to avoid damaging the plant. The more you pick, the more peas the plants will produce.

Tips

Peas are excellent plants for growing up a chain-link fence, and the taller varieties create a privacy screen quite quickly. The shorter and medium-height peas make interesting additions to hanging baskets and container plantings. They can grow up the hangers or supports or can be encouraged to spill over the edges and trail down.

Recommended

P. sativum var. *sativum* is a climbing plant with bright green, waxy stems and leaves and white flowers. The resulting pods are grouped into three categories: shelling peas, snow peas and snap peas. The seeds are removed from the pods of shelling peas and are the only part eaten. Snow peas are eaten as flat, almost seedless pods, often including the edible vine tips and newest leaves. Snap peas develop fat seeds, and the pod and seeds are eaten together. There is a wide array to choose from.

Shelling peas: **'Alaska'** is a heavy producer resistant to cold, pests and wilt. **'Green Arrow'** is a disease-tolerant heirloom boasting high yields, and it requires no support. **'Paladio'** produces big, easy-to-open pods in doubles, making for easy picking and shelling.

Snow peas: **'Snow Green'** has bears pods in multiples. The plants do not need support and are disease resistant. **'Mammoth Melting'** is an heirloom that produces huge pods. **'Oregon Sugar Pod II'** is a heavy yielder of tender, flat pods.

Snap peas: **'Sugar Ann'** is an All America Selections winner that bears rounded, fleshy pods. **'Sugar Lace'** is self-supporting, with sweet, stringless pods. **'Sugar Snap Cascadia'** is a dwarf, wilt-resistant variety bearing fleshy, crisp, rounded pods that remain tender and sweet for a long period.

Problems and Pests

Peas are prone to powdery mildew, so choose mildew-resistant varieties and avoid touching the plants when they are wet to prevent the spread of disease. Aphids and whiteflies can also cause problems.

Smooth-seeded peas are starchier and best used in soups, while wrinkled varieties are sweeter and generally eaten fresh.

Pepper

Capsicum

Features: bushy annual; attractive foliage; white flowers; colourful, edible fruit
Height: 20–60 cm **Spread:** 20–45 cm

The variety of sweet and chili peppers is nothing short of remarkable. Among the many different shapes, colours and flavours of peppers, there is sure to be one or two that appeal to you. A cool summer can really put a damper on fruiting, which can make hot pepper growing, in particular, a bit tricky in Canadian gardens.

Starting

Peppers need warmth to germinate and grow, and they take awhile to mature, so it is best to start them indoors 6–10 weeks before the last frost date. If you don't have ideal light conditions, your seedlings may become stretched out and do poorly even when moved to the garden. In this case, you may prefer to purchase started plants.

Growing

Peppers grow best in **full sun** in a warm location. The soil should be **average to fertile, moist** and **well drained**. Mulch to ensure the soil stays moist because most Canadians need to plant their peppers in a fairly hot garden location.

Most gardens will be hot enough to grow sweet peppers, but chili peppers need hotter weather to bear fruit. Try a dark mulch in a hot spot if you've had little luck with these peppers in the past.

'Banana'

Harvesting

Peppers can be picked as needed, once they are ripe. Chili peppers can also be dried for use in winter.

Tips

Pepper plants are neat and bushy. Once the peppers set and begin to ripen, the plants can be very colourful as the bright red, orange or yellow fruits contrast beautifully with the dark green foliage. They are a worthwhile addition to a hot, sunny border.

All peppers will do well in containers. Chili peppers in particular are suited to containers because they usually have the most interesting fruit shapes, and the containers can be moved indoors or to a sheltered spot to extend the season if needed. Some of the smaller chili peppers also make interesting houseplants for warm, sunny windows.

Recommended

C. annuum is the most common species of sweet and chili peppers. Plants are bushy with dark green foliage. Flowers are white, and peppers can be shades of green, red, orange, yellow, purple or brown.

Cultivars of sweet peppers include '**Big Bertha**,' '**Blushing Beauty**,' '**California Wonder**,' '**Carmen**,' '**Earlibird**' and '**Orange Sun**.' Some of the most tasty and beautiful sweet peppers are those in the **Fluo Series**. '**Mini Belle**' is a mix that is ideal for containers. Dwarf, compact plants produce large yields of small, blocky, sweet bell peppers in red, orange, purple or brown.

Cultivars of chili peppers include '**Anaheim**,' '**Cayenne**,' '**Jalapeño**,' '**Scotch Bonnet**' and '**Thai**,' just to name a few.

Banana peppers (Hungarian wax peppers) are more sweet than hot. '**Banana**' is an All America Selections winner ready in 70 days. The fruits are pale yellow when ripe and are vigorously produced.

C. chinense '**Habañero**' is one of the hottest chili peppers, native to the Caribbean.

Problems and Pests

Rare problems with aphids and whiteflies can occur.

Capsaicin is the chemical that gives peppers their heat. It is also the chemical used in pepper spray.

Soybean

Glycine

Features: bushy annual; attractive foliage; green, yellow or brown, edible seeds
Height: 30–90 cm **Spread:** 30–45 cm

These beans have been popular for years in Asian countries. One common preparation method involves simmering the beans in the pod in salted water. The seeds are then eaten out of the pods. We know them as edamame. The seeds are also excellent roasted.

Starting

Sow seeds directly into the garden after the last frost date has passed and the soil has warmed up. Seeds can be planted quite close together when space is at a premium, but ideally, give them 30–45 cm.

Growing

Soybeans grow best in **full sun** but tolerate some light afternoon shade. The soil should be of **average fertility** and **well drained**.

Harvesting

Soybean yields are very heavy. Harvest the beans when the pods are plump and full but the seeds are still tender and green. The pods can also be grown to maturity and the beans dried for use in soups and stews.

'**Manitoba Brown**' is a dark brown soybean that is incredibly vigorous and delicious, akin to the beans used in baked beans. '**Maple Amber**' is a Canadian soybean that is ready in 110 days, growing 90 cm tall and producing yellow seeds.

Problems and Pests
Leaf spot, bacterial blight, rust, bean beetles and aphids can cause problems.

Soybeans contain all nine essential amino acids, have no cholesterol and are low in saturated fats and sodium. They are an excellent source of dietary fibre and are high in iron, calcium, B vitamins, zinc, lecithin, phosphorus and magnesium.

Tips
Soybeans are ornamental, with attractive leaves and plentiful flowers. They can be used to make low, temporary hedges or planted in small groups in a border.

Recommended
G. max is a bushy annual that produces clusters of large-seeded pods. There are several soybean cultivars available. '**Beer Friend**' is used primarily for edamame. '**Black Jet**' matures in less than 100 days and is a favourite when seasoned with garlic, ginger, molasses and cumin as a snack. '**Butterbean**' is ready in 90 days bearing bushy plants 60 cm tall with delicious, green seeds. '**Karikachi No. 3**' is the ideal edamame soybean, ready in 90 days.

Squash

Cucurbita

Features: trailing or mounding annual; large, lobed, decorative leaves; colourful flowers and fruit **Height:** 45–60 cm **Spread:** 60 cm–3 m

Squash are generally grouped as summer and winter squash. The groupings reflect when we eat the squash more than any real difference in the plants themselves. Winter squash keep the longest and have the best flesh taste and texture when mature. Summer squash are tender and tasty when they are immature but tend to become stringy and sometimes bitter when they mature, and they don't keep as well.

Starting

Start seeds in peat pots indoors 6–8 weeks before the last frost date. Keep them in as bright a location as possible to reduce stretching. Plant out or direct sow after the last frost date, once the soil has warmed up. Plant on mounds of soil to ensure there is good drainage away from the base of the plant.

Generally, squash require 60–90 cm of space. If space is at a premium, some selections can be grown vertically, provided they have adequate support.

Growing

Squash grow best in **full sun** but tolerate light shade from companion plants. The soil should be **fertile, humus rich, moist** and **well drained**. Mulch well to keep the soil moist. Put mulch or straw under developing fruit of pumpkins and other

through a border of taller plants or shrubs. Small-fruited, trailing selections can be grown up trellises. All squash can be grown in containers, but the mound-forming and shorter-trailing selections are usually the most attractive.

Recommended

Squash plants are generally similar in appearance, with medium to large leaves held on long stems. Plants are trailing in habit, but some form short vines and appear to be more mound forming. Bright yellow, trumpet-shaped, male and female flowers are borne separately but on the same plant. Female flowers can be distinguished by their short stem and by the juvenile fruit at the base of the flower. Male flowers have longer stems. The fruits vary greatly in shape, size, texture and colour.

heavy winter squash to protect the skin while it is tender. Fertilize with compost tea or liquid fish fertilizer every 2–3 weeks.

Harvesting

Summer squash are tastiest when picked and eaten young. The more you pick, the more the plants will produce. Cut the fruit cleanly from the plant, and avoid damaging the leaves and stems to prevent disease and insect problems.

Winter squash should be harvested carefully, to avoid damaging the skins, just before the first hard frost. Cure them in a warm, dry place for a few weeks until the skins become thick and hard, then store them in a cool, dry place, where they should keep all winter. Check them regularly to be sure they aren't spoiling.

Tips

Mound-forming squash, with their tropical-looking leaves, can be added to borders as feature plants. The heavy-fruited, trailing types will wind happily

C. maxima includes buttercup squash, hubbard and kabocha. These plants generally need 90–110 days to mature. They keep well and have sweet, fine-textured flesh. '**Buttercup**' has a dark green rind with silvery grey lines, and dark yellow flesh that is sweet and nutty. '**Ambercup**' is a kabocha with streaked orange skin and orange flesh.

C. moschata includes butternut squash and generally needs 95 or more days to mature. These squash are good keepers. '**Butternut**' bears bottle-shaped, creamy brown fruits with dark yellow, nutty flesh. '**Butternut Supreme**' is bigger with higher yields.

C. pepo is the largest group of squash. Summer squash are ready to harvest in 45–50 days, and winter squash take from 70–75 days for acorn squash to 95–120 days for some of the larger pumpkins.

Summer squash: '**Defender**' is an early, medium-sized, disease-resistant zucchini. '**Black Forest**' is a climber, ideal for containers. It bears abundant dark green,

Squash generally need a long, warm summer to develop well. Gardeners in cooler areas should choose species and cultivars that mature in a shorter season.

cylindrical fruits. **'Midnight'** is compact and bushy, also perfect for containers. It produces spine-free stems and leaves for an easier harvest of the slightly speckled fruits. **'Sunny Delight'** is an early scallop or mini squash. It has bright yellow, thin, edible skin and tender flesh.

Winter squash: **'Big Max'** is a huge, round, pinkish orange pumpkin. **'Freaky Tom'** has a heavily warted, dark orange rind. **'Jack O'Lantern'** has a smooth, bright orange rind. **'Small Sugar'** is a sweet baking squash, maturing to 15–20 cm across. Acorn squash include **'Batwing Acorn,'** ready in 75 days with a patchy dark orange and green, rounded and ribbed rind, and **'Honeybear,'** a mini variety with dark green skin and sweet flesh.

Problems and Pests

Problems with mildew, cucumber beetles, stem borers, bacterial wilt and whiteflies can occur. Ants may snack on damaged plants and fruit, and mice will eat and burrow into squash for the seeds in fall.

Don't worry if some of your summer squash are too mature or your winter squash are not mature enough. Summer squash can be cured and will keep for a couple of months. They are still useful for muffins and loaves. Immature winter squash can be harvested and used right away; try them stuffed, baked or barbecued.

Tomato

Lycopersicon

Features: bushy or upright, annual vine; fragrant foliage; yellow flowers; colourful, edible fruit
Height: 45 cm–1.5 m **Spread:** 45–90 cm

Tomatoes are a delicious, nutrient-filled, sweet treat, and they are wonderful fresh off the vine. They are also quite possibly the easiest edible to grow. The hardest part will be choosing the variety because there is an almost endless array of fruit sizes, colours and flavours, so try a few each year until you find your favourites.

Starting

Start tomatoes indoors 6–8 weeks before the last frost date, or purchase them as started plants in spring. Plant seedlings and transplants deeply; bury the stem to the lowest set of leaves. Roots will form along the buried stem, which allows for extra growing power and support. Spacing varies for the different selections, so check the seed packet or plant tag for specifics.

Growing

Tomatoes grow best in **full sun**. The soil should be **average to fertile, humus rich, moist** and **well drained**. Keep tomatoes evenly moist to encourage good fruit production.

Except for the very small bush selections, tomatoes are quite tall and are prone to flopping over unless stakes, wire hoops, tomato cages or other supports are used.

Harvesting

Pick the fruit as soon as it is ripe. Tomatoes pull easily from the vine when they are ready. Tomatoes can also be picked green and ripened indoors, either left out in the open or placed in brown paper bags

'Brandywine'

baskets, particularly those varieties that produce cherry or grape tomatoes.

Recommended

L. lycopersicum are bushy or vine-forming annuals with pungent, bristly leaves and stems. Determinate plants grow to a specific height and are generally short enough to not need staking. Indeterminate plants continue to grow all summer and usually need staking. Clusters of yellow flowers are followed by fruit from midsummer through to the first frost. Fruits ripen to red, orange, pink, yellow or purple and come in many shapes and sizes. Beefsteak tomatoes produce the largest fruit, and cherry tomatoes produce the smallest. The following are only a few of the many tomato varieties to choose from.

Cherry tomato varieties: **'Sugary'** is an All America Selections winner that produces

When tomato plants were first introduced to Europe, they were grown as ornamentals, not for their edible fruit.

'Roma'

to speed up the process. Early picking is often necessary at the end of the season. It's important to harvest the fruits before a hard frost to prevent them from being damaged. Once picked, under-ripe tomatoes will keep indoors for weeks.

Tips

Tomatoes are bushy and have both attractive little flower clusters and vibrantly coloured fruit. Many of the selections grow well in containers and can be included in patio gardens and hanging

cherry tomatoes reminiscent of the Roma type, with orange-red skin. **'Black Cherry'** is an indeterminate tomato with blackish purple skin and dark red flesh. **'Honeybee'** is a bright yellow cherry tomato that is borne in clusters and ready in 60 days. **'Maskotka'** has dense, compact growth ideal for containers. The tiny fruits have a great resistance to cracking on ripening. **'Sungold'** is ready in 95 days, bearing thin-skinned, rich orange, bite-sized tomatoes in a cascading form. **'Tumbler'** is ready in 50 days, bearing fruits that tumble over the sides of containers on long stems. **'Moncherry'** is a mini cherry tomato producing heaps of little red fruits.

Standard varieties: **'Roma'** is a classic tomato. The fruits are pear to oval shaped with very few seeds. **'Principe Borghese'** is ready in 75 days, bearing meaty tomatoes, and does not require staking. **'Stupice'** is a high-yielding, indeterminate heirloom that can be harvested in 52–85 days, depending on how big you prefer the tomatoes to be. This variety is great in cooler weather.

'**Mortgage Lifter**' is another indeterminate heirloom that produces large, dark pink fruits with meaty flesh and few seeds.
'**Black Krim**' bears slightly flattened fruits with dark greenish black shoulders.
'**Lemon Boy**' produces fruits with yellow skin and flesh on an indeterminate plant.
'**Green Sausage**' is an elongated variety, green and yellow striped with green flesh.

Problems and Pests
Problems with tobacco mosaic virus, aphids, fungal wilt, blossom end rot and nematodes can occur.

Bush *is used interchangeably with* determinate *to describe plants with fruit that is set roughly all at once on short plants, whereas* vine *means* indeterminate, *or when fruit sets over a longer time on tall-growing plants.*

Arugula
Roquette, Salad Rocket
Diplotaxis, Eruca

Features: clump-forming, self-seeding, upright annual; toothed, peppery leaves
Height: 30–90 cm **Spread:** 15–30 cm

Some people consider this peppery annual to be a vegetable, others an herb. Arugula has experienced waves of popularity over the years. After close to two centuries of being overlooked, arugula is experiencing a new life in Canada, in particular as a salad green. The flowers and seeds are also edible. The flowers, which taste a little on the citrus side, can be used as an edible garnish.

Starting

Sow seed thinly once the risk of frost has passed. Seed crops in succession, once or twice per week throughout the growing season, to provide you with young, tender leaves from spring to fall. The seed germinates quickly, sprouting in just 3 days. Arugula is known to self-seed prolifically, so you may only have to seed it the one season.

Growing

Arugula prefers to grow in **full sun** or **partial shade. Cool, moist, rich** soil will help to produce more tender and less pungent leaves than those in dry, hot soil. Pinch the new leaves out frequently for use, and maintain a good level of moisture without keeping the soil too wet. Excessive fertilizer results in lush leaves lacking in flavour. Arugula can withstand light frosts.

E. vesicaria subsp. *sativa*

Harvesting

The leaves are aromatic, producing a peppery scent as they are harvested. They are most tender when picked before the flower stems emerge. They become more pungent and somewhat bitter over time. The leaves should always be used fresh, as drying diminishes the flavour. The leaves do not freeze well.

Tips

Arugula is best grown in a garden setting, in the ground, outdoors; however, it is possible to grow it in pots, either on the balcony or indoors. Make sure to sow the seed early in spring and use a bark compost potting mix. Arugula combines well with other herbs, including parsley, cilantro, basil, cress, dill and borage.

Recommended

D. tenuifolia (wild arugula) has a sharper flavour compared to the cultivated selections. It grows 30–40 cm tall. '**Discovery**' is a uniform, vigorous cultivar. It produces pungent leaves with a hint of sweetness in roughly 50 days from seed. '**Sylvetta**' grows into very dense, small bushes

loaded with deeply lobed leaves. The flowers are also delicious.

E. vesicaria **subsp.** *sativa* (salad arugula, salad rocket, roquette) is an upright annual with toothed leaves on tall stems tipped with white flowers that have purple veins. Slender, erect seedpods follow the flowers. It grows 60–90 cm tall but spreads only 15–20 cm. '**Astro**' is ready for harvest in 38 days, producing a more mild flavour and rounded leaves. '**Runway**' is a vigorous grower, producing large, deeply lobed leaves. '**Surrey**' is mature in 21 days for baby leaves, 40 days for full-sized leaves. This late-bolting cultivar is rich and spicy.

Problems and Pests

Flea beetles, cutworms, aphids and thrips can all prey on arugula, but rarely, and they're all easily treatable with a sharp spray of water or an insecticidal soap. Or, you can cover the emerging plants with a floating row cover.

The leaves can be added to stir-fries, pasta sauces, potato salad or almost any dish where spinach is used. In salads, arugula is tastefully complemented by nutty oil dressings.

Cress

Lepidium

Features: self-seeding annual; lacy, edible foliage
Height: 15 cm **Spread:** 15 cm

Cress is a group of botanically unrelated plants grown for their sharp, peppery or mustard-like flavour. Broad-leaf or curly cress (*Lepidium sativum*) and upland cress (*Barbarea verna*) are easier to grow than watercress (*Nasturtium officinale*), which requires very moist soil at all times. We're focusing on one of the selections, *L. sativum*, because of its strong peppery flavour and ease of growth.

Starting

Broadcast cress seed over the surface of the soil and cover lightly with soil or compost. Seed can be sown in early spring as soon as you can work the soil or in late summer through fall. Continuous crops will provide you with fresh cress all season long, but starting a crop in the middle of summer may cause the plants to produce flowers too quickly without making enough growth to harvest.

Growing

Cress thrives in **full sun to light shade** in soil that is very **moist, well drained** and of **average fertility**. Sow in all but the hottest months to prevent the plants from bolting or going to seed.

Harvesting

Cress is ready to harvest in as little as 15 days. To harvest, cut back plants halfway, and they will resprout before flowering. Cress is best used fresh.

Tips

Cress is suitable for a spot in your herb garden, but ensure that enough space is left for a succession of crops throughout the growing season. Cress can also be grown in containers. It is ideal for growing indoors year-round as a microgreen.

Recommended

L. sativum (broadleaf cress, curly cress) is a reseeding annual that produces deeply cut, lacy leaves on single, erect stems. Small, almost spherical flowers are produced only 3–4 weeks after sowing. **'Bubbles'** produces leaves with ruffled edges and blistered surfaces that are quite hot to

taste. This cultivar is also slower to bolt than others. **'Greek'** produces flat, dissected leaves that are spicy, sweet and nutty in flavour.

Problems and Pests

Cress selections rarely suffer from any pests, but mildew can be a problem during excessively hot days if your plant dries out completely or during consistently wet weather.

Cress is invaluable in salads, sandwiches and garnishes for its spicy flavour and finely curled, nutritious leaves. It is the perfect complement to egg dishes, including omelettes and quiche. Cress soup has an unusual and unique flavour. Cress can also be used as a substitute for spinach in dishes where a stronger flavour is required.

Dandelion

Taraxacum

Features: clump-forming, self-seeding annual; edible leaves, flowers and roots
Height: up to 30 cm **Spread:** up to 15 cm

The time has come to embrace the dandelion. Dandelions have been used medicinally for thousands of years, and they've been a staple in certain cuisines for almost as long. Every part of the plant can be used, clearly they're easy to grow and they're even attractive. If you're willing to try one new thing this year, make it dandelions.

Starting

Dandelions can be sown outdoors 4–6 weeks before the last frost. Sow seed directly, and once they've sprouted above the soil, thin so they are 15–20 cm apart.

Dandelions readily reseed themselves, but often in places where you'd rather they didn't grow.

Growing

Dandelions prefer **full sun** but will clearly grow in just about any light. It doesn't really matter what type of soil they have, whether the drainage is adequate, or anything else for that matter. These plants are incredibly resilient and tolerant of poor conditions. Add liberal amounts of compost to areas you're sowing if you plan on harvesting the roots.

Harvesting

A few weeks before harvesting the leaves, cover the plants with a dark, opaque fabric to block out most of the light, which will blanch the leaves, reducing the bitterness. The youngest leaves are the least bitter and most flavourful. Tender leaves can be picked throughout the growing season.

Pick the flowers when they are bright yellow. Use them fresh, making sure to remove the whole stem. To prevent the flowers from closing after cutting, place them in a bowl of cold water until just before eating or serving them.

The roots can be harvested at any time and roasted and ground for later use.

Tips

Dandelions can be added to your herb garden, or they can be grown in a block or row in your vegetable garden. Dandelions

The leaves are delicious in salads and are a fine substitute for spinach. The crowns are a delicacy when deep-fried, and the roots can be used as a coffee substitute after being roasted and ground. The flowers have many uses, including for wine and fresh in salads. Unopened flower buds are tender and tasty, and they offer a crunch in green salads.

can also be directly sown into containers for harvest closer to the kitchen, with the advantage that the container will keep them from spreading out of control.

Recommended

T. officinale produces long, deeply toothed leaves and deep yellow flowers on tall, hollow stems. The brightly coloured flowers quickly change to fluffy, airy seed heads that are easily taken by the first summer breeze. Over time, dandelions develop a deep and somewhat extensive root system. '**Thick-leaved Improved**' produces a tender, thicker leaf with less bitterness. '**Verte de Montgomery**' is similar. Also consider using the wild varieties in your yard, which are probably just as tasty.

Problems and Pests

Dandelions are generally problem free.

Do not eat dandelions that have been in contact with lawn fertilizers, herbicides or any other chemical contaminants.

Kale, Collards & Mustard Greens

Brassica

Features: tender biennial; decorative, smooth or wrinkled, green, bronze or purple, edible leaves **Height:** 45–75 cm **Spread:** 45–60 cm

Mustard variety

These nutrient-packed, leafy cabbage and broccoli siblings are some of the most decorative members of the Brassica family. This grouping is growing steadily in popularity. The nutrient content, flavour, texture and pure versatility are second to none.

Starting
All three of these plants can be sown directly into the garden as soon as the soil can be worked in spring; a light frost won't harm them. You may wish to make several successive plantings of mustard because the leaves have the best flavour when they are young and tender.

Growing
These plants grow best in **full sun**. The soil should be **fertile, moist** and **well drained**. Mustard in particular should not be allowed to dry out, or the leaves may develop a bitter flavour.

Harvesting
Because the leaves are what you will be eating, you don't have to wait very long after planting to start harvesting. Once plants are established, you can start harvesting leaves as needed. Pick a few of the outer leaves from each plant.

Collard variety

Tips

These plants make a striking addition to beds and borders, where the foliage creates a good complement to plants with brightly coloured flowers. The smaller varieties can be grown in containers, either on the balcony or indoors.

Recommended

B. oleracea var. *acephala* (collards; Scotch kale, curly-leaved kale) and *B. oleracea* var. *fimbriata* (Siberian kale, Russian kale) are the kales and collards; however, the common names are not always used consistently.

Kale: 'Blue Curled' and 'Blue Ridge' have good flavour and vigour, and 'Dwarf Blue Curled' is good for containers. 'Improved Dwarf Siberian' maintains its quality long after other selections have bolted. 'Red Russian' is an heirloom that produces tender, sweet, green leaves with red spines. It is a good container selection. 'Curly Green' is great even when flowering. 'Tuscan' ('Dinosaur,' 'Lacinato') is not only tasty but also beautiful; it bears long, strap-like, blistered, dark green to almost black leaves, and it is another good container selection.

Collards: 'Green Glaze' is often referred to as "greasy greens." 'Flash' is an early variety with smooth leaves that is slow to bolt. 'Hi-Crop' has crinkled, blue-green leaves and is also bolt resistant. 'Blue Max' is disease resistant. 'Champion' bears rich green leaves in a compact form.

B. juncea subsp. *rugosa* (mustard) forms large clumps of ruffled, creased or wrinkled leaves in shades of green, bronze or purple. 'Mizuna' ('Japonica') has mild, finely cut, curled leaves. 'Mibuna' has mild, lance-shaped leaves. It is mature in 40 days, but the baby leaves can be harvested at 20 days. 'Savanna' produces large, thick, deep green, savoury but mild leaves. 'Florida Broadleaf' is an heirloom with sharp-flavoured, smooth leaves with white midribs. 'Red Giant' produces spicy, maroon leaves with light green midribs.

Problems and Pests

Problems with cutworms, leaf miners, caterpillars, root maggots, cabbage white butterfly larvae, white rust, downy mildew and powdery mildew can occur. Avoid planting any Brassica in the same spot in successive years.

Collards were some of the earliest cultivated forms of Brassica oleracea. The Romans brought them to Britain in 400 BCE, where they became known as Coleworts.

Kale variety

Lettuce & Mesclun

Letuca

Features: clump-forming annual; decorative, edible leaves
Height: 15–45 cm **Spread:** 15–45 cm

Lettuce, with its undulating or rippled edges and variable leaf colours, is an ornamental treasure trove that deserves a spot in the garden even if you don't care for salad. Mesclun, whether a spicy or a mild blend, makes a welcome addition to salads and stir-fries while providing a good groundcover in the garden.

Starting

Lettuce and mesclun can be started directly in the garden around the last frost date. The seeds of leafy lettuces and mesclun can be scattered across a prepared area and do not have to be planted in rows, but you may wish to be more selective when planting head lettuces so you don't have to thin the plants out as much later.

If you make several smaller plantings spaced 1–2 weeks apart, you won't end up with more plants than you can use maturing at once. For an earlier crop,

Romaine variety

Loose-leaf lettuce and mesclun can be harvested by pulling a few leaves off as needed or by cutting an entire plant 5–10 cm above ground level. Most will continue to produce new leaves even if cut this way.

Tips

Lettuce and mesclun make interesting additions to container plantings, either alone or combined with other plants. The loose-leaf types and mesclun mixes are also well suited to growing indoors.

In beds and borders, mesclun makes a decorative edging plant. All lettuces and mesclun are fairly low growing and should be planted near the front of a border so they will be easier to get to for picking.

To add a twist to your mesclun mixes, try adding a few herb seeds; cilantro, dill, parsley and basil are a few you may enjoy.

start a few plants indoors about 4 weeks before you plan to plant them outdoors.

Growing

Lettuce and mesclun grow well in **full sun, light shade** or **partial shade** in a sheltered location. The soil should be **fertile, moist** and **well drained**. Add plenty of compost to improve the soil, and be sure to keep your lettuce moist. Lettuce is prone to drying out in hot and windy situations, so it is best to plant it where it will get some protection. Plants under too much stress can quickly bolt and go to seed or simply wilt and die.

Harvesting

Head-forming lettuce can be harvested once the head is plump. If the weather turns very hot, you may wish to cut heads earlier because the leaves develop a bitter flavour once the plants go to flower.

Recommended

L. sativa forms a clump of ruffle-edged leaves and comes in many forms.

Loose-leaf lettuce forms a loose rosette of leaves rather than a central head. There are many varieties available. '**Grand Rapids**' is ready in 45 days, producing large, frilly, bright green leaves that are tender and sweet. This variety is vigorous and slow to bolt. '**Prizehead**' produces loose, crumpled leaves edged with reddish brown in 45–55 days and has a buttery flavour. '**Red Salad Bowl**' produces mild-flavoured, loose, deeply cut, deep burgundy leaves in a rosette form and is slow to bolt. '**Simpson Elite**' is mature at 50 days but can be harvested at 30–45 days. It is incredibly vigorous, with a delicate flavour.

Butterhead lettuce forms a loose head and has a very mild flavour. '**Bibb**' produces a loose head of buttery leaves with a distinctive flavour. This selection matures in 57 days but will bolt in hot weather. '**Esmeralda**' has a sweet flavour and succulent texture and is resistant to bolting and pests. '**Yugoslavian Red Butterhead**' is an heirloom variety bearing 30 cm heads covered in red-tinged outer leaves surrounding an almost white centre, with a mild flavour.

Romaine lettuce has a more upright habit, and the heads are fairly loose but cylindrical in shape. '**Baby Star**' is a mini romaine that is ready in 65–85 days, producing dark green, shiny leaves with a creamy white heart.

Crisphead or iceberg lettuce forms a tight head of leaves. '**Early Great Lakes**' is ready

'Bibb'

Butterhead variety

in 65–85 days, with bright green outer leaves and creamy white inner leaves. **'Ithaca'** produces tightly wrapped, crisp heads with great vigour. **'Summertime'** is a later, compact variety and is slow to become bitter.

Mesclun mixes can be a combination of different lettuces, usually loose-leaf types, eaten while very young and tender. Mixes often also include other species of plants, including mustard, broccoli, radicchio, endive, arugula, chicory and spinach. Most seed catalogues offer a good selection of pre-mixed mesclun as well as separate selections to create your own mix. The mixes are often ready in 40–65 days, in balanced blends of spicy, mild and sweet. The colour and texture of the leaves are quite varied, making for a beautiful salad.

Problems and Pests
Problems with root rot, leaf spot, flea beetle and mosaic virus can occur.

An essential tip for successful lettuce from the garden is to use a floating row cover for protection against pests and, in some cases, to prevent tip burn in the hot summer sun.

Microgreens

Various species

Features: cotyledon and first true leaves of a plant; nutritionally dense; very flavourful
Height: 3–8 cm **Spread:** 1–3 cm

There's no such thing as a microgreen seed; pretty much any edible plant can be grown as a microgreen because a microgreen is simply a plant harvested at the first stage of growth. Microgreens are nutritionally dense and extremely flavourful, packing a lot of punch for their size, and they are very easy to grow; it's a win-win-win situation. Choose a variety of seeds for your microgreen garden to suit your personal tastes.

Starting

Prepare a seed tray with a shallow layer of loose soil. Generously sprinkle seeds over top; do not cover them with soil. Lightly water; then cover with a dish towel or an empty tray to block the light. Once the seeds have sprouted, remove the cover.

Growing

Microgreens are easist to grow **indoors**, with **6 to 8 hours of light** each day. They prefer **loose, moist, well-drained** soil.

Mix in compost and a small amount of vermiculite. Once growth starts, water daily, being careful not to flatten the delicate stems if watering from above.

Harvesting

Most microgreens are ready for harvest in 1–2 weeks; some take 3–4 weeks. When they're ready, simply cut them just above soil level with scissors. If not using them right away, they can be stored in a sealed, preferably glass, container and will keep for up to 2 weeks in the refrigerator.

Tips

Microgreens don't need a lot of space or depth and will grow in just about any shallow pot or tray. Group seeds with similar maturing times together to make harvesting easier.

Recommended

Beta vulgaris **subsp.** *cicla* (Swiss chard) has a mild, beet-like flavour and colourful stems. **'Ruby Red'** has red stems, and

'Bright Lights' produces a mix of red, white, pink, yellow, orange and purple stems.

Brassica juncea **subsp.** *rugosa* (mustard) has a spicy, zesty flavour. **'Mizuna'** has interesting leaves and a milder flavour.

Brassica oleracea **var.** *fimbriata* (kale) is excellent as a microgreen. **'Red Russian'** has sweet, green leaves with red spines.

Eruca vesicaria **subsp.** *sativa* (arugula) has a distinctive, spicy flavour and purple stems.

Ocimum basilicum (basil) has superb flavour when harvested as a microgreen. **'Dark Opal'** is a purple variety, good for visual interest.

Problems and Pests

Pests are not usually a problem indoors. However, poor air circulation and/or overwatering can lead to mould.

If you notice tiny white threads around your seeds, don't worry; it isn't mould. They're just root hairs, and they're a sign that your plants are healthy.

Sorrel

Rumex

Features: clump-forming perennial; oblong, edible leaves
Height: 15–90 cm **Spread:** 30–60 cm

Sorrel is a hardy perennial that, once established, will appear each spring without fail. Sorrel can be classified somewhere between a salad green and an herb. The tangy, sour leaves are a perfect addition to a salad of mixed greens, but the leaves can also be used to flavour soups, marinades and egg dishes.

Starting

Sow seed directly in the garden in fall or spring. Sorrel self-seeds if flowering spikes are not removed.

R. acetosella

Growing

Sorrel grows well in **full sun** or in **light** or **partial shade**, especially in hotter parts of Canada. The soil should be **average to fertile, acidic, humus rich, moist** and **well drained**, but this plant is fairly adaptable. Mulch to conserve moisture. Once it is established, divide sorrel every three or four years to keep the plant vigorous.

Harvesting

Pick leaves as needed in spring and early summer. Remove flower spikes as they

R. acetosa

emerge to prolong the leaf harvest. Once the weather warms up and the plant goes to flower, the leaves lose their pleasant flavour. If you cut the plant back a bit at this point, you will have fresh leaves to harvest in late summer and fall when the weather cools again.

Tips

Sorrel is a tasty and decorative addition to the vegetable, herb or ornamental garden. French sorrel makes an attractive ground-cover and can be included in mixed containers.

Recommended

R. acetosa (garden sorrel, broad-leaf sorrel) is a vigorous, clump-forming perennial. The inconspicuous flowers are borne on a tall stem that emerges from the centre of the clump. It grows 45–90 cm tall and spreads about 30 cm. ***R. acetosella*** (sheep sorrel) is smaller, with a little less acidity.

R. scutatus (French sorrel, buckler-leaf sorrel) forms a low, slow-spreading clump of foliage. The leaves are stronger tasting but not as plentiful as those of garden

sorrel and it tolerates heat better. It grows 15–45 cm tall and spreads up to 60 cm.

Problems & Pests

Snails, slugs, rust and leaf spot can cause rare problems.

Oxalic acid gives sorrel leaves their flavour, and though they are safe to eat, in large quantities they can cause stomach upset.

Spinach

Spinacia

Features: clump-forming annual; smooth or crinkled, edible leaves
Height: 30–45 cm **Spread:** 15–25 cm

Nutritious and versatile, spinach is useful in a wide variety of dishes. And it's effortless to grow, so you might want to consider adding this popular, leafy plant to your garden, even if you don't grow any other vegetables. In fact, it grows with ease in containers, with or without ornamentals, so give it a try.

Starting

Direct sow spinach in spring as soon as the soil can be worked. Space the seeds 20–25 cm apart. Several successive sowings in spring and again in mid- to late summer will provide you with a steady supply of tender leaves.

A young spinach plant can tolerate a light frost, but if temperatures are expected to fall below -5° C, you should cover it.

Growing

Spinach grows well in **full sun** or **light shade** and prefers cool weather and a cool location. The soil should be **fertile, moist** and **well drained**.

Add a layer of mulch to help keep the soil cool because this plant bolts in hot weather. Most Canadian gardeners won't have to worry about bolting because our cool summer nights are ideal for growing spinach, but bolt-resistant varieties are also available.

Harvesting

Pick leaves, as needed, a few at a time from each plant. The flavour tends to deteriorate as summer heats up and the plant matures and goes to flower.

Tips

Spinach's dark green foliage is attractive when mass planted and provides a good contrast for brightly coloured flowers. Try it in a mixed container that you keep close to an entryway to make harvesting more convenient. It can also be grown indoors in winter for a year-round supply.

Recommended

S. oleracea forms a dense, bushy clump of glossy, dark green, smooth or crinkled (savoyed) foliage. Plants are ready for harvest in about 45 days. **'Bloomsdale'** produces dark green, deeply savoyed foliage. **'Correnta'** is a smooth-leaved variety with tender, dark green leaves. **'Scarlet'** is a smooth-leaved variety with dark red veins. **'Tyee'** is a semi-savoy variety that is bolt resistant. **'Fiorana'** is an early variety, great for successive plantings throughout the growing season. **'Regal'** is well suited to dense plantings and is ideal as baby spinach. **'Unipack 151'** is a slightly later variety, ready in 50 days. It is a semi-savoy spinach with dark green, tender but thick leaves. **'Catalina'** is the most popular for indoor growing. Its deep green leaves are very flavourful, and it is quick growing.

Problems and Pests

Avoid powdery and downy mildew by keeping a bit of space between each plant to allow for good airflow.

Smooth-leaved spinach has thin, tender, sweet leaves, while savoy-leaved spinach has broader, thicker, crinkled leaves that hold up better when cooked.

Sprouts
Various species

Features: roots or shoots of sprouted seeds; nutritionally dense
Height: N/A **Spread:** N/A

Mung bean

Sprouts are an excellent way to eat fresh, homegrown produce even in the dead of winter. They may be tiny, but they are packed with nutrition. Plus, they're quick and easy to grow.

Starting
All you need to get started is a glass canning jar, some muslin or cheesecloth to use as a filter and some sprout seeds. Place a tablespoon of seeds in the jar and add warm (not hot) water to cover; swirl the seeds around and then drain the water. Add more warm water until it is about 5 cm above the seeds. Secure the filter over the opening and place the jar in a cool, dark place to let the seeds soak for about 12 hours (up to 24 hours for larger seeds).

Growing
After the soaking period, drain the water. Add enough water to swirl the seeds (later sprouts) around, then drain again before placing the jar back in its cool, dark place. Repeat the rinsing process twice a day, morning and night, being sure to drain all the water each time; sprouts should stay moist but should not sit in water.

Harvesting

Sprouts will be filling your jar and ready to eat in 3 to 6 days (onion sprouts take longer). Rinse them well and store them loosely in an airtight container in the refrigerator for up to a week.

Tips

Sprouts do not require light or soil. However, if you want the tips to green up, expose them to a few hours of light before you pick them.

Recommended

Allium cepa (onion) sprouts have a tangy, subtle onion flavour with interesting black tips. The seeds take up to 2 weeks to sprout.

Brassica oleracea* var. *botrytis (broccoli) goes from seed to sprout in 3–6 days. The sprouts have a mild peppery taste.

Alfalfa

Lens culinaris (lentil) sprouts are ready in 3 days. The large, yellow seeds produce light green sprouts.

Medicago sativa (alfalfa) sprouts have a mild, nutty taste and are ready in 5–6 days.

Vigna radiata (mung bean) is the most popular sprout worldwide. The creamy, fat sprouts are ready in 3–5 days.

Problems and Pests

Sprouts are susceptible to bacterial growth, including *E. coli*. It is important to keep the growing environment sterile; use clean equipment, and wash your hands before you handle the jar or sprouts. Smell your sprouts before you eat them; a bad odour is often an indicator of bacteria. When in doubt, throw them out.

Onion

Not every vegetable makes a good sprout. Members of the potato family (including tomatoes, peppers and eggplants) are poisonous as sprouts.

Swiss Chard

Beta

Features: biennial grown as an annual; glossy, green, edible leaves with colourful stems and ribs **Height:** 20–45 cm **Spread:** 30 cm

Swiss chard is one of the most useful vegetables to include in your garden. The tasty leaves and stems can be harvested all summer, and the wide range of colours makes it a valuable ornamental addition to beds, borders and even container gardens.

Starting
The corky, wrinkled seed of Swiss chard is actually a dried fruit that contains several tiny seeds. Plant the seed fruits directly in the garden around the last frost date. You will probably have to thin the plants a bit even if you space the seeds 7–15 cm apart because several plants can sprout from each fruit.

Growing
Swiss chard grows well in **full sun** or **partial shade**. It grows best in cool weather. The soil should be **fertile, moist** and **well drained**. Mulch lightly with compost to maintain moisture and improve soil texture.

Harvesting
Swiss chard matures quickly, and a few leaves can be plucked from each plant every week or so all summer. You can generally start picking leaves about a month after the seed sprouts and continue to do so until the plant is killed back by frost.

'Bright Lights'

striped, with green or bronze foliage; **'Fordhook Giant,'** a white-stemmed heirloom; **'Gazelle,'** which produces a contrast of dark green leaves with deep red stems and veins, all in 58 days; **'Lucullus,'** with light green, crumpled, curly leaves and broad stems with rounded, white ribs; **'Orange Fantasia,'** with orange stems; **'Perpetual,'** a heat-resistant, non-bolting cultivar with small, pale green stems and spinach-like leaves; **'Rainbow,'** with a combination of red, orange, yellow or white stems; **'Rhubarb,'** with bright red stems; and **'Silverado,'** with creamy white stems.

Problems and Pests
Rare problems with downy mildew, powdery mildew, leaf miners, aphids, caterpillars and root rot can occur.

If you find that chard fades out in your garden during the heat of summer, you can plant a second crop in midsummer for fresh leaves in late summer and fall.

Tips
Chard has decorative foliage. Although the leaves are usually glossy green, the stems and veins are often brightly coloured. When planted in small groups in your borders, chard adds a colourful touch. The bushy, clumping habit also makes it well suited to mixed container plantings, as well as indoor plantings as long as you give it room to grow and enough light.

Recommended
B. vulgaris subsp. *cicla* forms a clump of usually green, but also purple, red or bronze, glossy leaves that are often deeply crinkled or savoyed. Stems and veins may be pale green, white, yellow, orange, pink, red or purple. Popular cultivars include **'Bright Lights,'** an All America Selections winner that produces a colourful mix of stems, mostly solid but occasionally

'Rainbow'

Blackberry

Rubus

Features: thicket-forming shrub; long, arching canes; spring flowers; summer fruit
Height: 1–3 m **Spread:** 1.2–1.5 m

The sweet, juicy berries of these shrubs are popular for use in jams, pies and other fruit desserts, but they are just as delicious when eaten fresh. Blackberries have long, flexible canes, and though they can stand freely without staking, they may take up less room if they are kept tidy by being loosely tied to a supportive structure such as a stout post or fence.

Starting

Bare-root canes should be purchased in late winter or early spring and should preferably be planted while they are still dormant. Container-grown plants are often available all season, though they may not establish as well.

Growing

Blackberries grow well in **full sun, light shade** or **partial shade**, though the best fruiting occurs in full sun. The soil should be of **average fertility, humus rich, moist** and **well drained**. These plants prefer a location **sheltered** from strong winds. Blackberries are prone to winter damage.

followed by red or black berries in late summer. Thornless varieties are available. **'Prime-Ark 45'** is a flavourful, thorny variety that is hardy to zone 4, which makes it a good container candidate; the hardier the shrub, the easier it will be to overwinter. (Zones 5–8)

Problems and Pests
Problems with anthracnose, powdery mildew, rust, fire blight, leafhoppers and caterpillars can occur.

Blackberries and raspberries are closely related. Because colour is not a surefire indicator of species, the easiest way to tell them apart is to pick them; raspberries are hollow, but blackberries come off the bush with their core intact.

Prune out some of the older canes each year once plants become established to keep plants vigorous and to control the spread.

Harvesting
Pick fruit as soon as it is ripe in mid- to late summer. The fruit does not all ripen at once, and you can harvest it for a month or more.

Tips
These shrubs form rather formidable thickets and can be used in shrub and mixed borders, along fences and as hedges.

Blackberries can be grown in containers, provided you have a large enough container and are prepared to overwinter them.

Recommended
R. fruticosus forms a thicket of thorny stems or canes. Canes can grow up to 3 m long, and thickets can spread 1.5 m or more. White, or occasionally pink, late spring or early summer flowers are

Blueberry

Vaccinium

Features. attractive, deciduous shrub; small, bell-shaped, white or pink flowers; edible fruit
Height: 10 cm–1.5 m **Spread:** 30 cm–1.5 m

These attractive bushes are low and spreading or rounded and upright. The leaves turn a beautiful shade of red in fall. These plants are an admirable addition to any border, with the added asset of delicious summer fruit.

Starting
Plants can be purchased and planted at any time, as long as the ground is workable. The best selection is generally in spring.

Growing
Blueberries grow well in **full sun, partial shade** or **light shade**. The soil should be of **average fertility, acidic, moist** and **well drained**. They grow best in areas where the soil is acidic and peaty or sandy. Soil can be amended, but plants never grow as well in alkaline soil. Little pruning is required.

Harvesting
Blueberries are ready for harvesting when they turn, not surprisingly, blue. Test one, and if it is sweet and tastes the way you expect, they are ready for harvest.

Tips
If you have naturally acidic garden soil, blueberries make an excellent choice for

a fruit-bearing shrub in a woody or mixed border. They are hardy in many Canadian gardens and make interesting low hedges.

Dwarf varieties can be grown in containers, as long as you are prepared to overwinter them. Lowbush varieties can even be tried in window boxes.

Recommended

V. angustifolium var. *laevifolium* (lowbush blueberry, wild blueberry) is a low, bushy, spreading shrub with small, glossy, green leaves that turn red in fall. It grows 10–60 cm tall and spreads 30–60 cm. Clusters of small, bell-shaped, white or pink flowers are produced in spring, followed by small, round fruit that ripens to dark blue in midsummer. (Zones 2–8)

V. corymbosum (highbush blueberry) is a bushy, upright, arching shrub with green leaves that turn red or yellow in fall. It grows 90 cm–1.5 m tall with an equal spread. Clusters of white or pink flowers at the ends of the branches in spring are followed by berries that ripen to bright blue in summer. Several cultivars are available. '**Bluecrop**' has tart, light blue berries. '**Blueray**' has large, dark blue berries. '**Chippewa**' has sweet, light blue berries and is

compact and hardy enough for containers. '**Top Hat**' is a lowbush/highbush dwarf hybrid. It grows 30–60 cm tall with an equal spread and was developed for containers. (Zones 3–8)

Problems and Pests

Rare problems with caterpillars, rust, scale, powdery mildew and root rot can occur.

A handy way to preserve blueberries is to spread them on a cookie sheet and put them in the freezer. Once they are frozen, they can be transferred to an air-tight bag. The berries will be frozen individually, rather than in a solid block, making it easy to measure out just what you need for a single recipe or serving.

Currant

Ribes

Features: shrub with long, arching, sometimes prickly stems; attractive lobed leaves; yellow, pink or red, often fragrant flowers; edible fruit **Height:** 45 cm–1.8 m **Spread:** 45 cm–1.5 m

Currants are quite varied, available in red, white and black. The berries, mainstays in colonial cookery, are making a comeback in the "current" (sorry!) trend toward local-harvest, seasonal cuisine.

Starting

Plants can be purchased and planted in fall or early in spring. When planting, dig a hole of sufficient volume to allow the roots to be fully extended. Be careful to set the plant at its previous soil mark, or just below.

Growing

Currants grow and fruit best in **full sun**, but they don't mind some shade from intense afternoon heat. The soil should be **average to fertile, moist** and **well drained**. They prefer a sheltered location.

These long-lived shrubs will survive a considerable amount of neglect, but for good berry production, regular maintenance is key. A thick mulch helps maintain cool roots. Weed carefully to avoid damaging the relatively shallow roots. Annual pruning is a good idea; cut away old wood at ground level.

Harvesting

Berries ripen in mid- to late summer but will require several pickings because they do not ripen all at the same time. For ease of picking, gather currants in clusters, not individually. A fork, used gently, makes a great tool for later stripping the clusters. Berries will keep several days in the refrigerator and also make wonderful preserves and jams.

Tips

Currants, with their attractively coloured berries—red, soft yellow or rich black—can be included in a woody mixed border or added to the vegetable garden.

Currants will also do well in a container; keep in mind that as the plant grows, so should the container.

Currants shine in northern climates, enjoying, as they do, a good dose of frost and winter cold for the best fruit production.

Recommended

R. nigrum (black currant) grows to 1.5 m tall with an equal spread and has fragrant foliage and glossy, black berries. It is not quite as long-lived as red or white currants. The dwarf **'Ben Sarek'** is both prolific and mildew-resistant, and it is a good choice for a container. The Canadian-developed varieties **'Consort,' 'Coronet'** and **'Crusader'** are considered blister rust resistant. (Zones 3–8)

R. rubrum (red currant, white currant) grows 90 cm–1.8 m tall, with a 60 cm–1.5 m spread, and has small berries, with the colour depending on the variety. **'Jonkheer van Tets,'** an early variety of red currant cultivated commercially in the Netherlands, is mildew resistant. **'Red Lake'** is more flavourful and produces large, red berries. **'Stanza'** is a compact red variety. The white currant **'White Imperial'** is a small, upright shrub. The larger **'White Versailles'** produces sweet, pale yellow fruit. Many cooks consider the grape-flavoured white currant tastier than the milder red currant. (Zones 3–8)

Problems and Pests

Birds, aphids, mildew, blight and rust are potential problems.

Elderberry

Sambucus

Features: large, bushy, deciduous shrub; edible flowers and fruit
Height: 1.5–4.5 m **Spread:** 1.5–4.5 m

Elderberry is very hardy, tolerates most soil conditions and requires little care. It can, in fact, be a little too easy to grow; it has a tendency to spread, either by seed or sucker. With its creamy flowers and clusters of smoky purple berries, though, it can be an attractive addition to the wilder parts of the garden.

Starting
Elderberries can be purchased and planted in spring. They will send up new suckers every spring; these can be left to grow or be pruned out if you are short on space.

Growing
Elders grow well in **full sun** or **partial shade**. The soil should be of **average** fertility, **moist** and **well drained**. These plants tolerate dry soil once established, but appreciate a layer of mulch.

With its suckering habit, elderberry can look untidy without regular pruning. Prune out branches more than 3 years old in late winter.

Harvesting
The flowers can be picked soon after opening and used fresh or dried.Berries are harvested in early fall and are easy to pick from the upright, thornless shrub. At this point they can be frozen and brought out later in winter, when the busy harvest season is over, to make into preserves or pies.

S. canadensis

Tips

Elders can be used in a shrub or mixed border, in a natural woodland garden or next to a pond or other water feature. They can be pruned to fit smaller spaces.

Recommended

S. canadensis (sweet elder, American elder) is a deciduous, hardy shrub growing 1.5–3 m tall, with a similar spread, and is the preferred choice for berries. Sprays of tiny, white, star-like flowers are followed by clusters of small, dark purple berries. '**Aurea**' has yellow leaves, fragrant flowers and red fruit. (Zones 3–8)

S. nigra (European elder, black elder) is a rounded shrub with white flowers followed by dark purple berries. It grows up to 4.5 m tall and wide. '**Black Beauty**' has dark foliage that get blacker as the season progresses, and pink flowers. '**Laciniata**' has deeply dissected leaflets that give the shrub a feathery appearance. '**Madonna**' has dark green foliage with wide, irregular margins. '**Pulverulenta**' has dark green and white mottled foliage. (Zones 4–8)

Problems and Pests

These plants are pretty much pest free, except for a little competition from birds.

Both the flowers and the fruit can be used to make wine. The berries are popular for pies and jelly. The raw berries are marginally edible but not palatable and can cause stomach upset, particularly in children. All other parts of elders are toxic.

S. nigra 'Madonna'

Goji Berry
Wolfberry
Lycium

Features: spiny shrub forming a dense thicket of arching branches; white and mauve, trumpet-like flowers; orange-red, fall berries **Height:** 1–4 m **Spread:** 1–2.5 m

Goji, touted for its health properties and long history in traditional Chinese medicine, is advertised as reputedly benefiting a list of ailments including arthritis, diabetes, heart disease and cancer. The seedy, grape-size berries are said to have slight overtones of tomato and taste somewhat like a sweet cranberry.

Starting
Seeds and plants are available online if your regular nursery or garden centre does not carry them. The adventuresome grower can also try germinating seed from dried goji. Plant seeds or plants in pots or directly into the garden in spring.

Growing
Goji prefers **full sun**. For best fruiting results, a full 8 hours of sunlight is recommended. The soil should be **rich** with lots of organic matter, **moist** and **well drained**. Use a shallow mulch, and water in the early morning; avoid wetting the leaves.

Harvesting

Flowers set throughout summer, and the berries should be ready to pick by late fall. Gather berries when they've gone from green to red and have a sweet taste. They are usually dried before being eaten. Shoots and leaves may also be harvested and used as a leafy vegetable.

Tips

Goji is considered an adaptable plant with reports of it surviving freezing temperatures as well as conditions of high heat and humidity. It can be grown in containers, given enough protection over winter.

Recommended

L. barbarum (Tibetan goji, Mongolian goji), often advertised as a Himalayan berry, also grows in China. Both light purple and white, trumpet-shaped flowers begin in summer and continue until frost. The flowers develop into small, oval, red berries containing varying numbers of tiny, yellow seeds. (Zones 4–9)

L. chinense (Chinese wolfberry) is similar and is sometimes marketed as goji berry. Its appearance, habit and growing requirements are the same as for goji, though it may not grow quite as tall. (Zones 5–9)

L. europeaum may have a slightly more upright shape than the other two species, but with an almost identical appearance, it is often mistaken for either of the other two species, a typical problem for all three plants. Growing conditions are the same as for goji. (Zones 5–9)

Problems and Pests

Goji appears relatively pest free. Slugs and deer can take a liking to it, though. Wet leaves may cause fungal problems.

Goji has not only been cultivated in Asia for centuries but has also been grown in Britain since the 1700s.

Gooseberry

Ribes

Features: shrub with long, arching, sometimes prickly stems; attractive lobed leaves; yellow, pink or red, often fragrant flowers; edible fruit **Height:** 45 cm–1.5 m **Spread:** 45 cm–1.8 m

Gooseberry produces a tart fruit that varies from pale green to yellow to pinkish purple when fully ripe. Gooseberries are popular in Europe, where they are used in everything from soup to wine. Give them a try; you'll soon discover just how good these underrated berries can be.

Starting

Plants can be purchased and planted in fall or very early in spring. When planting, dig a hole of sufficient volume to allow the roots to be fully extended. Be careful to set the plant at its previous soil mark, or just below.

Growing

Gooseberries grow and fruit best in **full sun**, but they don't mind some shade from intense afternoon heat. The soil should be **average to fertile, moist** and **well drained**. They prefer a sheltered location. A trellis will improve air circulation, make harvesting easier and allow for more plants in a smaller space.

These long-lived shrubs will survive a considerable amount of neglect, but for good berry production, regular maintenance is key. A thick mulch helps maintain cool roots. Weed carefully to avoid damaging the relatively shallow roots.

Annual pruning is a good idea; cut away old wood at ground level.

Harvesting

Berries ripen in mid- to late summer but will require several pickings because they do not ripen all at the same time. Gooseberries can be stripped from the branch with a gloved hand and the debris winnowed later. Gooseberries often last for up to 2 weeks in the refrigerator and also make wonderful preserves and jams.

Tips

The gooseberry, with its inconspicuous blossoms and green fruits, tends to blend into surrounding vegetation and is often unfairly relegated to a forgotten corner of the backyard.

The small varieties are a good choice for containers; keep in mind that as the plant grows, so should the container.

Recommended

R. uva-crispa fruits best in areas that are likely to experience frost, of which Canada has no shortage. **'Invicta'** bears a heavy crop of large fruit. **'Pixwell'** is a hardy variety with shorter thorns than most, with the advantage that the fruit tends to hang away from the thorns. **'Jubilee'** is a compact, disease-resistant variety with large, red, tasty berries. **'Golden Drop'** is a yellow-skinned dessert variety with a neat habit. (Zones 3–8)

Problems and Pests

Birds, aphids, mildew, blight and rust are potential problems.

Gooseberry and currants are often implicated in white pine blister rust. The rust requires both the pine and a Ribes species to complete its life cycle. The disease does little harm to the berry bush but is lethal to the pine. If you garden in a white pine area, certain varieties of currant and gooseberry may be prohibited.

Highbush Cranberry
American Cranberrybush
Viburnum

Features: bushy or spreading, deciduous shrub; spring flowers; attractive summer and fall foliage; edible fruit **Height:** 1.5–4.5 m **Spread:** 1.5–3.6 m

The highbush cranberry, variously called pimbina or pembina, is a member of the varied and prolific viburnum family that includes the snowball tree and the Korean spice bush. The edible but tart fruit is popular for making jellies, pies and wines.

Starting
Purchase plants and transplant them into the garden any time during the growing season.

Growing
Highbush cranberries grow well in **full sun** or **partial shade**. The soil should be of **average fertility, moist** and **well drained**. These plants tolerate both alkaline and acidic soils.

Little pruning is needed. Remove awkward, dead, damaged or diseased branches as they occur. Fruiting is better when more than one plant of a species and of a different cultivar is grown.

Harvesting

Pick the ripe fruit in fall. It can be sweetened somewhat by freezing or by picking it after the first frost or two.

Tips

Highbush cranberries can be used in borders and woodland gardens. They are a good choice for plantings near patios, decks and swimming pools as privacy screens.

Recommended

V. opulus var. *americana* (*V. trilobum*) is a dense, rounded, deciduous shrub native to much of central North America. Early summer clusters of showy sterile and inconspicuous fertile flowers are followed by edible, red fruit. The fall colour is red. This species is resistant to aphids. '**Compactum**' is a smaller, denser shrub that grows 1.5–1.8 m tall and wide. Its flowers and fruit resemble those of the species. (Zones 2–7)

Problems and Pests

Aphids, borers, dieback, downy mildew, grey mould, leaf spot, mealybugs,

powdery mildew, scale insects, treehoppers, *Verticillium* wilt, weevils and wood rot can affect highbush cranberries.

*Although cranberry sauce is traditionally made with the fruit of the American cranberry (*Vaccinium macrocarpon*), the fruit of highbush cranberries makes an acceptable alternative. The large seeds must be strained out of the highbush cranberry sauce.*

'Bailey Compact'

Raspberry

Rubus

Features: thicket-forming shrub; long, arching canes; spring flowers; summer fruit
Height: 1–1.5 m **Spread:** 1.2 m or more

Sweet, juicy raspberries are popular for use in jams, pies and other fruit desserts, but they are just as delicious when eaten fresh. Thickets are often pruned and staked to form neat rows but can be left to spread freely if you have the space.

Starting
Bare-root canes should be purchased in late winter or early spring and should preferably be planted while they are still dormant. Container-grown plants are often available all season, though they may not establish as well.

Growing
Raspberries grow well in **full sun, light shade** or **partial shade**, though the best fruiting occurs in full sun. The soil should be of **average fertility, humus rich, moist** and **well drained**. These plants prefer a location **sheltered** from strong winds.

Prune out some of the older canes each year once plants become established to keep plants vigorous and to control the spread.

Harvesting
Pick fruit as soon as it is ripe in mid- to late summer. The fruit does not all ripen at once, and you can harvest it for a month or more. Some raspberry varieties are ever bearing and produce fruit in flushes from midsummer through fall.

bearing and ever-bearing. Although raspberry shrubs are perennial, the canes are biennial, generally growing the first year and producing fruit the second. In the third season, the cane dies back. Ever-bearing canes begin to fruit late in the season of their first fall, then again the second summer. They are suitable where fall is long and warm; summer-bearing varieties are more suitable for short-season areas. **'Autumn Bliss'** is an ever-bearing variety with well-behaved, somewhat compact canes suitable for containers. **'Heritage'** is a more cold-hardy ever-bearing variety. (Zones 3–8)

Problems and Pests
Problems with anthracnose, powdery mildew, rust, fire blight, leafhoppers and caterpillars can occur.

If you have more raspberries than you can use fresh, a handy way to preserve them is to spread them on a cookie sheet and put them in the freezer. Once they are frozen, they can be transferred to an airtight bag. The berries will be frozen individually, rather than in a solid block, making it easy to measure out just what you need for a single recipe or serving.

Tips
These shrubs form rather formidable thickets and can be used in shrub and mixed borders, along fences and as hedges.

Raspberries, particularly ever-bearing varieties, can be grown in containers, provided you have a large enough container and are prepared to overwinter them.

Recommended
R. idaeus forms a thicket of bristly stems or canes. Canes grow 1–1.5 m long, and thickets can spread 1.2 m or more. White, spring flowers are followed by red, yellow, black or purple fruit in midsummer. Raspberries fall into two categories: summer-

Serviceberry
Saskatoon, Juneberry
Amelanchier

Features: single- or multi-stemmed, deciduous large shrub or small tree; spring or early summer flowers; edible fruit; fall colour **Height:** 1.2–9 m **Spread:** 1.2–9 m

A. canadensis

Serviceberres are first-rate North American natives, and breeders have refined the habits to make them more useful in home landscaping. They bear lacy, white flowers in spring, followed by edible berries. In fall, the foliage colour ranges from a glowing apricot to deep red. Artistic branch growth showing in winter makes these shrubs excellent all year long.

Starting
Seedlings can be purchased and planted in spring. Once established, the shrubs will send up suckers each spring.

Growing
Serviceberry grows well in **full sun** or **light shade**. The soil should be **fertile, acidic, humus rich, moist** and **well drained**, though serviceberry will tolerate alkaline soil and adjust to drought.

Very little pruning is needed. Young plants, particularly multi-stemmed ones, can be pruned to encourage healthy, attractive growth and form; only the strongest, healthiest stems should be allowed to remain. Dead, damaged, diseased and awkward branches can be removed as needed.

Harvesting

The fruit ripens all at once in midsummer, facilitating one major picking. The fruit can be used in the place of blueberries in any recipe, having a similar, but generally sweeter flavour.

Tips

Serviceberries make beautiful specimen plants or even shade trees in small gardens. The shrubby forms can be grown along the edge of a woodland or in a border and are especially attractive in a naturalized planting.

Smaller species can be grown in large containers with winter protection.

Recommended

A. alnifolia (western serviceberry, saskatoon) is a suckering shrub that grows up to 4 m tall and spreads 3 m. White, spring flowers are followed by sweet, juicy, summer berries. **'Regent'** is a smaller cultivar, growing 1.2–1.8 m tall with an equal spread. (Zones 3–8)

A. canadensis

A. arborea (downy serviceberry, juneberry) forms a small, single- or multi-stemmed tree. It grows 4.5–7.5 m tall and spreads 4.5–9 m. Clusters of fragrant, white flowers are borne in spring. The edible berries ripen to reddish purple in summer. In fall, the foliage turns to shades ranging from yellow to red. (Zones 4–8)

A. canadensis (shadblow serviceberry) forms an upright, suckering shrub. It grows 2–6 m tall and spreads 1.5–4.5 m. White, spring flowers are followed by edible, dark purple fruit in summer. The foliage turns orange and red in fall. This species tolerates moist, boggy soil conditions. (Zones 3–8)

Problems and Pests

Problems with rust, fire blight, powdery mildew, leaf miners, borers and leaf spot can occur but are generally not serious.

A. alnifolia

Birds are attracted to the ripening fruit and may eat all the berries before you get a chance to pick any.

Strawberry

Fragaria

Features: spreading perennial; soft, bright green leaves; white, sometimes pink flowers; bright red, edible fruit **Height:** 15–30 cm **Spread:** 30 cm or more

Many of these plants, with their pretty little flowers, spread vigorously by runners. Long shoots spread out from the parent plant, and small baby plants grow at the tips. Purchasing just a few plants in spring will quickly provide you with plenty of fruit-producing plants by the end of summer.

Starting
Some selections can be started indoors about 12 weeks before you plan to plant them outside. Other selections are only available as crowns or plants. Plant them outdoors around the last frost date. They tolerate light frosts.

Growing
Strawberries grow well in **full sun** or **light shade**. The soil should be **fertile, neutral to alkaline, moist** and **well drained**. These plants tolerate acidic soil but don't produce as much fruit.

Harvesting
Pick strawberries as soon as they are ripe. Some types produce a single large crop of

Similar in appearance, they generally form a low clump of three-part leaves and may or may not produce runners. Flowers in spring are followed by early to mid-summer fruit. Some plants produce a second crop in fall, and others produce fruit all summer. The fruit of wild or alpine strawberries is smaller than the fruit of the other two species. Popular cultivars include mid-season producers '**Cabot**' and '**Kent**' and ever-bearing producers '**Sweetheart**,' '**Temptation**' and '**Tristar**.' (Zones 3–8)

Problems and Pests

Strawberries are susceptible to fungal diseases, so a mulch is recommended as a layer between the soil and fruit. Plants are fairly problem free, though some leaf spot, spider mite and wilt problems can occur.

fruit in early summer, and others produce a smaller crop throughout most or all of summer.

Tips

Strawberries make interesting, tasty, quick-growing groundcovers. They do well in containers, window boxes and hanging baskets. The selections that don't produce runners are also good for edging beds.

Recommended

F. chiloensis (Chilean strawberry), *F. vesca* (wild strawberry, alpine strawberry) and *F. virginiana* (Virginia strawberry) have been crossed to form many hybrids.

The origin of the name strawberry is uncertain, perhaps originally being "strayberry" or "strewberry." It is certain, however, that the name has nothing to do with the practice of mulching the plants with straw to protect the fruit from dirt and fungal diseases.

Apple

Malus

Features: rounded, mounded or spreading, small to medium, deciduous tree; white, pink or purple, spring flowers; edible fruit in late summer or fall **Height:** 2–15 m **Spread:** 1–15 m

'Spartan'

Apples have been developed and rated for many desirable traits in both the tree and the fruit. Trees can be bred for qualities such as plant size, disease resistance, abundance of fruit and cold hardiness. Fruit may be soft or firm when cooked, sweet or tart to the taste, long lasting for storage or shorter lasting for quick eating, and early or late ripening. Your best bet is to select disease-resistant plants with the traits you are most interested in and that will grow best in your area.

Starting

Plant new trees in spring once the soil has warmed.

Growing

Apples grow best in **full sun** but tolerate partial shade with some reduction in fruiting. Choose a **sheltered** location because cold winds can damage flowers in spring, reducing fruit set. The soil should be **average to fertile, slightly acidic, moist** and **well drained**. Plants perform poorly in excessively sandy, rocky or alkaline soils. Clay soils are tolerated as long as they do not stay wet for extended periods of time. Fruiting may be delayed in wet soils that take a long time to warm up in spring.

Apple trees don't actually need to be pruned, but fruit production and even ripening can be greatly improved through good pruning practices.

Harvesting

Apples ripen from late summer to late fall, depending on variety and climatic conditions.

Tips

With the advent of readily available dwarf stock, an apple tree of one's own is entirely possible for even the smallest home garden. Apples can also be trained as espaliers for growing against a fence or wall.

Several varieties of apples can even be grown in containers. Columnar apples tend to stay compact in containers because the container restricts their root growth, but they yield a lot of fruit.

Recommended

M. x domestica is a variable group of hybrids that range in habit from columnar to open and spreading. **'Ambrosia'** is hardy with a crisp-fleshed fruit that is low in acidity. **'Cortland'** is an older variety of dessert apple with a somewhat squat shape and very white flesh. **'Empire'** is known for its deep, almost maroon skin and doesn't bruise easily. **'Gala'** is an elegant dessert apple with a pronounced sweetness and is a good candidate for storage. **'MacIntosh,'** the quintessential Canadian apple, has good colour and a crunchy bite when fresh. **'Northern Spy'** matures in mid- to late fall and is often used for pies

and cider. **'Spartan,'** another Canadian star, is the first apple developed within a formal scientific breeding program. If you can't decide, it is possible to purchase stock with several varieties of apples grafted onto a single tree. (Zones 3–8)

Problems and Pests

Birds, aphids, wasps, coddling moths, scab, powdery mildew, canker and rot can cause problems.

Apple trees perform poorly, bearing little or no fruit, when they don't have a sufficient dormant period in winter. This is rarely, if ever, a problem in Canada.

Espalier specimen

Cape Gooseberry

Ground Cherry

Physalis

Features: trailing or creeping, tender perennial grown as an annual; yellow, blue or white, small flowers; edible, ornamental fruit **Height:** 1 m **Spread:** 1 m

Cape gooseberry got its name in the early 19th century when the small, juicy, golden fruit, with its crisp, paper-like husk, was exported from the Cape of Good Hope. The pricey and uncommon fruit is now more likely to be shipped from New Zealand or China.

Starting

For best results, start plants indoors as you would tomatoes. Transfer seedlings outside once the weather warms up in spring.

Growing

Cape gooseberries do best in **full sun**. Light shade is tolerated with somewhat reduced fruiting. The soil should be of **average fertility, moist** and **well drained**. Plants need a long, warm growing season to develop colour. Pinch out new shoots to encourage bushy growth.

Harvesting

The papery husk that surrounds each fruit turns beige or light brown when the fruit

is ripe. Fruit in the husk can be stored for up to three months.

Tips

Cape gooseberries grow well in pots, especially the small *P. pruinosa* varieties. Cape gooseberries can also be included in the

P. peruviana

vegetable garden or a naturalistic border where their rustic, casual appearance will be appreciated.

Recommended

P. peruviana is a tender, tropical perennial with a brighter yellow berry encased in a long, pointed calyx. **'Golden Berry'** produces rich-tasting fruit. **'Giant Poha Berry'** grows 30–75 cm tall and has fuzzy, sage-coloured leaves.

P. pruinosa (dwarf cape gooseberry) is an annual with hairy stems and hairy calyxes. **'Aunt Molly,'** developed in Poland, has good flavour for eating fresh or making jam. **'Little Lantern'** is an especially small, compact plant with a spreading habit. Its dull yellow berries are often described as tasting slightly like pineapple.

Problems and Pests

If flea beetles are a problem, try crop row covers.

Physalis, a member of the nightshade family, includes the tomatillo (P. ixocarpa) and the Chinese lantern plant (P. alkekengi), with its decorative orange husks.

Cherry

Prunus

Features: upright, rounded, spreading or weeping, deciduous tree or shrub; spring to early summer flowers; edible fruit **Height:** 1.5–18 m **Spread:** 1.5–10 m

Like many other fruits, cherries have the best flavour when picked fresh compared to store-bought. Sweet cherries are not hardy in many parts of Canada, but several of the tart or sour cherries are.

Starting

Cherries can be purchased as bare-root stock or in containers. Plant them in spring to give them a growing season to become established.

In general, two different cultivars of sweet cherries that bloom at the same time are needed for pollination to occur, though there are a few self-fertile cultivars available.

Growing

Cherries grow best in **full sun**. The soil should be of **average fertility, moist** and **well drained**. Shallow roots will emerge from the ground if the tree is not getting sufficient water.

Pruning should be done after flowering. Remove damaged growth and wayward branches as required.

Harvesting

Cherries ripen from midsummer to fall, depending on the variety. The birds will begin to snack on them before they are quite ripe enough for you to pick.

P. avium

P. tomentosa

Tips

Cherry species are beautiful as specimen plants, and many are small enough to be included in almost any garden. The smallest ones can even be grown in large containers with winter protection.

Small species and cultivars can also be included in borders or grouped to form informal hedges or barriers.

Recommended

P. avium (sweet cherry) is an upright, deciduous tree with red bark and dark green leaves that turn red or yellow in fall. Clusters of white flowers in spring are followed by bright red fruit in mid- to late summer. It can grow to 18 m tall, with a spread half that much. This is the species from which most of the sweet cherry cultivars have been developed. **'Bing'** is a well-known sweet cherry. **'Stella'** was the first self-fertile sweet cherry to be developed. **'Compact Stella'** makes an excellent container specimen. (Zones 3–8)

P. cerasus (sour cherry) is a rounded, spreading, deciduous tree. Clusters of white, spring flowers are followed by bright red fruit. It grows about 4 m tall,

with up to an equal spread. **'Evans'** and **'Montmorency'** are popular cultivars. **'Morello'** is a hardy variety that tolerates shade. (Zones 2–8)

P. tomentosa (Nanking cherry) is a dense, spreading shrub with slightly hairy, serrated foliage. White or pinkish, spring flowers are followed by red fruit that ripens in late summer or fall. It grows 2–3 m tall and spreads to 5 m. (Zones 2–7)

Problems and Pests

The many possible problems include aphids, borers, caterpillars, leafhoppers, mites, nematodes, scale insects, canker, crown gall, fire blight, powdery mildew and viruses. Root rot can occur in poorly drained soils. Stress-free plants are less likely to have problems.

Although most cherries have edible flesh, the pits, bark and leaves contain hydrocyanic acid and are toxic.

P. tomentosa

Grape

Vitis

Features: woody, climbing, deciduous vine; attractive foliage; late summer to fall fruit
Height: 7–15 m **Spread:** 7–15 m

We usually think of grape vines only for their wine-producing fruit, but their fast-growing nature, dense habit and attractive foliage make them ideal for quickly creating privacy barriers and providing shade for porches. Let them do multiple duty in your garden, providing fruit, shade and privacy.

Starting

Bare-root stock should be purchased in late winter or early spring and should preferably be planted while it is still dormant. Container-grown plants may also be available.

Growing

Grapes produce best in **full sun**, but the plants tolerate partial shade. The soil should be **moist, acidic** and **well drained**. Grapes tolerate most well-drained soil conditions.

Trim grape plants to fit the space you have, in mid-winter and again in mid-summer. If you wish to train a grape more formally, cut the side shoots back to within two or three buds of the main stems. Such pruning encourages flowering and fruiting.

Harvesting

The phrase "grape harvest" conjures up romantic images of crisp, fall days and post-harvest feasts in the vineyard on checked tablecloths, but really it's as straightforward as waiting until the grapes are ripe (browning of the stems of the bunches is a good indicator) and then snipping the bunches. Scissors are great

grower to see what grapes will grow best in your garden. (Zones 5–8)

Problems and Pests

Diseases and pests to watch for include downy mildew, powdery mildew, canker, dieback, grey mould, black rot, root rot, leaf spot, grape leaf skeletonizer, scale insects and mealybugs. These problems are not likely to be as serious in a garden with only one or two plants as they are in a vineyard.

Grape leaves can be used in cooking, such as in Middle Eastern dolma, for which grape leaves are used as wrappers to contain a savoury rice mixture.

for this. Your biggest concern will be watching out for bees or, depending where you live, feasting bears. If you have a cool, humid cellar, fresh grapes, stored in a single layer, should keep for months.

Tips

Grape vines can be trained to grow up and over almost any sturdy structure. They may need to be tied in place until the basic structure is established. Grow them up walls, over fences, up porch rails, on pergolas or arbours or almost anywhere else.

Recommended

V. vinifera (wine grape) is a woody climber best known for the wine grapes it produces. It makes an attractive addition to the garden and bears edible fruit. Several varieties have been developed for cooler or shorter summers; check with your local nursery or contact a specialty

Hardy Kiwi

Actinidia

Features: woody, climbing, deciduous vine; early summer flowers; edible fruit
Height: 4.5–9 m **Spread:** indefinite

A. arugata variety

Hardy kiwi is handsome in its simplicity. Its lush green leaves, vigour and adaptability make it useful, especially on difficult sites. The straight green of that species with blotches of pink and white added create the attractive variegated kiwi. Nursery catalogues make a convincing case for planting variegated kiwi—there is nothing else quite like it in the twining world. But it really doesn't perform like the pictures when it comes right out of the pot. A few years' maturity helps produce variegation, and very hot weather and shade will reduce it.

Variegated kiwi does not grow as rampantly as hardy kiwi.

Starting

Purchase bare-root or container-grown plants in spring and plant them out once the last frost date has passed.

Growing

Kiwi vines grow best in **full sun** or **partial shade**. The soil should be **fertile** and **well drained**. These plants require shelter from strong winds.

Prune in late winter. Plants can be trimmed to fit the area they've been given, or, if greater fruit production is desired, side shoots can be cut back to two or three buds from the main stems. Kiwi vines can grow uncontrollably. Don't be afraid to prune them back if they are getting out of hand.

Harvesting
The fruit can be picked in late summer or fall.

Tips
These vines need a sturdy structure to twine around. Pergolas, arbours and sufficiently large and sturdy fences provide good support. Given a trellis against a wall, a tree or some other upright structure, kiwis will twine upward all summer. They can also be grown in containers placed near some sort of climbing support.

A. arugata (this page)

Recommended
A. arguta (hardy kiwi, bower actinidia) grows 6–9 m tall but can be trained to grow lower through the judicious use of pruning shears. The leaves are dark green and heart shaped. White flowers are followed by smooth-skinned, greenish yellow, edible fruit. (Zones 3–8)

A. kolomikta (variegated kiwi vine, kolomikta actinidia) grows 4.5–6 m tall. The green leaves are strongly variegated with pink and white, and some of the leaves may be entirely white. White flowers are followed by smooth-skinned, greenish yellow, edible fruit. (Zones 4–8)

Problems and Pests
Kiwis are occasionally afflicted with fungal diseases, but these are not a serious concern.

The fruits of A. arguta *and* A. kolomikta *are hairless and high in vitamin C, potassium and fibre. These species make good local substitutes for* A. chinensis (A. deliciosa)*, the commercially available brown, hairy-skinned kiwi.*

Melon

Cucumis

Features: trailing annual vine; attractive foliage; yellow flowers; large, edible fruit
Height: 30 cm **Spread:** 1.5–3 m

Success with melons is somewhat limited in most Canadian gardens; they prefer warmer summer weather and a longer growing season than we can provide them. They are worth trying, though, and in the right spot, they can do really well.

Starting

Melons can be started indoors about 6 weeks before you want to transplant them to the garden. They don't like to have their roots disturbed, so plant them in fairly large peat pots so they have plenty of room to grow and can be set directly into the garden once the weather warms up.

If you aren't sure how well melons will grow in your garden, try the short-season selections and plant them in the warmest part of the garden.

Growing

Melons grow best in **full sun** in a warm location. The soil should be **average to fertile, humus rich, moist** and **well drained**. Fruit develops poorly with inconsistent moisture, and plants can rot

in cool or soggy soil. Use raised beds or mound the soil up before planting to improve drainage. The fruit will be sweeter and more flavourful if you cut back on watering as the fruit is ripening.

Harvesting

Melons should be allowed to fully mature on the vine. Muskmelons develop more netting on the rind as they ripen. They generally slip easily from the vine with gentle pressure when ripe. Honeydew melons develop a paler colour as they ripen. They must be cut from the vine when they are ripe.

Tips

Melons have attractive foliage and can be left to wind through your ornamental beds and borders.

Melons can also be grown in containers and, if they are placed near a fence or trellis, trained to grow up rather than out. As the fruit becomes larger, you may need to support it so the vines don't get damaged.

You can create hammocks out of old nylon pantyhose to support the melons.

Recommended

C. melo subsp. *reticulatus* (muskmelon) and *C. melo* subsp. *indorus* (honeydew melon) are tender annual vines with attractive, green leaves. Bright yellow flowers are produced in summer. Male and female flowers are produced separately on the same vine. The melons are round, green or gold in colour and some, usually muskmelons, develop a corky tan or greenish netting as they ripen. Muskmelons generally develop orange or salmon-coloured flesh, and honeydew melons develop pale green or yellow flesh. Most melons take 70–85 days to produce mature, ripe fruit. Popular cultivars include 'Alaska,' 'Earlidew,' 'Earlisweet,' 'Fastbreak,' 'Gourmet' and 'Passport.'

Problems and Pests

Powdery mildew, *fusarium* wilt, cucumber beetles and sap beetles can be quite serious problems. Mildew weakens the plants, and the beetles may introduce wilt, which is fatal to the plants.

When maturity dates are given for fruits and vegetables, they usually refer to optimum conditions. Cool weather can greatly delay the development of your melons. Choose short-season varieties, but anticipate that you may need a longer season than suggested.

Rhubarb

Rheum

Features: clump-forming perennial; red or green stems; large, deeply veined leaves; spikes of flowers in summer **Height:** 60 cm–1.2 m **Spread:** 90 cm–1.8 m

Rhubarb treads the fine line between fruit and vegetable. We usually eat it in fruit dishes and think of it more as a fruit, but rhubarb is actually a vegetable. All you really need to know is that it is extremely easy to grow and delicious in pies, crumbles and cakes.

Starting
Purchase crowns in spring. Or, if friends or neighbours have a rhubarb plant, ask them for a division from their plant.

Growing
Rhubarb grows best in **full sun**. The soil should be **fertile, humus rich, moist** and **well drained**, but this plant adapts to most conditions. Gently work some compost into the soil around the rhubarb each year, and add a layer of compost mulch. A fertile soil encourages more and bigger stems.

Rhubarb can stay in one spot for many years, but it will be more vigorous and productive if divided every 8 to 10 years. Dig it up in early spring while it is still dormant. Divide the crown into several sections, making sure that each section contains at least one bud or "eye." Replant one or two sections and compost or give the rest away.

Harvesting

Begin picking rhubarb once the stalks are large enough to use and roughly the width of your finger. Harvest the stems by pulling them firmly and cleanly from the base of the plant. Cut the leaves from the stems and compost or spread them around the base of the plant as mulch. Rhubarb's flavour is better earlier in summer, and harvesting generally stops by late July or early August, when the stems start to become dry, pithy and bitter.

Do not harvest the stalks in the first year. Let the plant develop an established root system first. Harvest sparingly the second year—not more than half of the stalks. In the third and subsequent years, harvest freely.

Although the flowers are quite interesting and attractive, remove them to prolong the stem harvest.

Tips

With its dramatic leaves, bright red stems and intriguing flowers, rhubarb will look good in a corner of the vegetable garden or in an ornamental bed.

Rhubarb will also grow well in a large container, but it will need to be divided twice as often as it would in the ground.

Recommended

R. rhabarbarum and *R.* x *hybridum* form large clumps of glossy, deeply veined,

green, bronzy or reddish leaves. The edible stems can be green, red or a bit of both. Spikes of densely clustered, red, yellow or green flowers are produced in midsummer. Popular varieties include '**Colossal**,' with huge leaves and stems, '**Crimson Cherry**,' with bright red stalks, and '**Victoria**,' with greenish leaf stalks that mature to a combination of red and green. '**Canada Red**' is popular throughout the country because of its flavour, hardiness, colour and texture. It bears deep red, tender stalks. (Zones 2–8)

Problems and Pests

Rhubarb rarely suffers from any problems.

Only the stems of rhubarb are edible. The leaves contain oxalic acid in toxic quantities.

Watermelon

Citrullus

Features: climbing or trailing, annual vine; yellow flowers; large, decorative, edible fruit
Height: 30 cm **Spread:** 1.5–3 m

Tasty and juicy, watermelon is the ultimate summer treat. Make it an even bigger treat and try growing your own. It grows best in hot, humid weather, but plenty of short-season varieties are available for Canadian gardeners.

Starting

Watermelon requires a long growing season and should be started indoors 4–6 weeks early in individual peat pots. Started plants can also be purchased at garden centres and nurseries. Transplant them into the garden after the last frost date and once the soil has warmed up.

Growing

Watermelon grows best in **full sun**. The soil should be **fertile, humus rich, moist** and **well drained**. This plant likes plenty of water during the growth and early fruiting stages, but to intensify the flavour, it should be allowed to dry out a bit once the fruit is ripening.

Harvesting

A watermelon is generally ready to pick when the pale white area on the skin where the fruit sits turns yellow. Some experimentation may be required before you become adept at judging the ripeness of the fruit.

Tips

Small-fruited watermelons make an attractive climbing specimen for patio containers, though even the small fruits may need some support as they grow. This plant can also be left to wind through ornamental beds and borders.

Recommended

C. lanatus is a trailing vine that takes 65–105 days to mature. The fruit skin may be light green with dark green stripes or solid dark green. The flesh may be red, pink, orange or yellow. Popular early maturing cultivars include **'Gypsy,' 'New Queen,' 'Sugar Baby'** and **'Yellow Doll.'**

Problems and Pests

Problems with powdery mildew, *fusarium* wilt, cucumber beetles and sap beetles can occur. Watermelon fruit blotch is a serious problem that can affect this plant, but not usually in Canada.

Watermelon is native to tropical parts of Africa, though it was introduced to Asia and has been grown there for centuries.

Basil

Ocimum

Features: bushy annual; fragrant, decorative leaves; white or light purple flowers
Height: 30–60 cm **Spread:** 30–45 cm

'Genovese' and 'Cinnamon'

The sweet, fragrant leaves of basil add a delicious, licorice-like flavour to salads and tomato-based dishes. Grow it where you won't forget to use it, either in a sunny spot on the patio or even in the kitchen by a bright window.

Starting
Basil is easy to start from seed. Start seeds indoors about 4 weeks before the last frost date, or sow seed directly outdoors once the last frost date has passed and the soil has warmed up. Press seeds into the soil and sift a little more soil over them. Keep the soil moist. Generally seeds will germinate within a week.

Growing
Basil grows best in a **warm, sheltered** location in **full sun**. The soil should be **fertile, moist** and **well drained**. Pinch the flowering tips regularly to encourage

bushy growth and leaf production. Mulch soil to retain water and to keep weeds down.

Harvesting

Pluck leaves or pinch back stem tips as needed. Basil is tastiest if used fresh, but it can be dried or frozen for use in winter.

Tips

Some of the purple-leaved varieties are very decorative and make fine borders. Although basil grows best in a warm spot outdoors, either in the ground or in a container, it can be grown successfully indoors in a pot by a bright window, providing you with fresh leaves all year.

Recommended

O. basilicum is a bushy annual or short-lived perennial with bright green, fragrant leaves. It bears white or light purple flowers in mid- to late summer. There are many cultivars of basil, with varied leaf sizes, shapes, colours and flavours. '**Green Globe**' forms a rounded mound of tiny leaves. '**Mammoth**' has huge leaves, up to

'Siam Queen'

25 cm long and about half as wide. '**Purple Ruffles**' has dark purple leaves with frilly margins. '**Siam Queen**' is a cultivar of Thai basil with dark green foliage and dark purple flowers and stems. Try '**Scented Trio**' from Renee's Garden, a three-pack of seeds including '**Cinnamon,**' citrus-scented, lemon-flavoured '**Mrs. Burns**' and garnet-coloured '**Red Rubin.**'

Problems and Pests

Fusarium wilt is probably the worst problem that afflicts basil.

Basil makes a great companion for tomatoes because they both require warm, moist growing conditions and are delicious when eaten together.

Bay Laurel

Laurus

Features: tender, evergreen shrub; aromatic foliage
Height: 30 cm–1.2 m **Spread:** 20–60 cm

Bay leaves are commonly used in soups and stews. Bay laurel is an undemanding plant that is happily transferred from a sunny window indoors to a lightly shaded spot outdoors when the weather allows.

Starting
Bay laurel can be started from seed, but germination may take up to 6 months. Plant the seeds in warm soil and keep the environment warm and moist, but not wet or the seeds will rot. It is simpler to purchase started plants, which are available from specialty growers and nurseries.

Growing
Bay laurel grows well in **full sun** or **partial shade**. A plant that will be moved indoors for winter should be grown in partial or light shade in summer. The soil should be **fertile, moist** and **well drained**. This plant is shallow-rooted and can dry out quickly in hot or windy weather. Mulch to reduce evaporation.

In winter, move bay laurel indoors and keep it in a cool but sunny room; continue to water it regularly, as needed.

Harvesting
It may take a couple of years before your bay laurel is leafy enough to be used regularly. Pick fresh leaves as needed to use in cooking. Leaves can be dried and stored for later use, but this plant is evergreen, so you should be able to pick fresh leaves all year.

Recommended
L. nobilis is a bushy, evergreen shrub. It grows up to 12 m tall in the Mediterranean, where it is native. In containers, it can be kept to a more manageable size. Plants rarely flower in Canada. **'Aureus'** is a cultivar with golden yellow foliage.

Problems and Pests
Rare problems with scale insects and mealybugs can occur, but these are usually easy enough to wash or rub off smaller plants. Powdery mildew can occur in poorly ventilated situations.

Laurel is a traditional symbol of victory.

Tips
Bay laurel is best grown in containers in Canada because the plants need to be brought indoors during freezing weather. It makes an attractive addition to patios, decks and the steps of a staircase with other potted herbs, vegetables and flowers.

Chives

Allium

Features: clump-forming, self-seeding perennial; edible foliage; mauve, pink or white, edible flowers **Height:** 20–60 cm **Spread:** 30 cm or more

The delicate onion flavour of chives is best enjoyed fresh. Mix chives into dips, or sprinkle them on salads and baked potatoes. The blooms are striking in the garden and in salads and herbal vinegars.

Starting

Chives can be started indoors 4–6 weeks before the last frost date or planted directly in the garden. They also can be purchased as plants.

Growing

Chives grow best in **full sun**. The soil should be **fertile, moist** and **well drained**, but chives adapt to most soil conditions. Plants self-seed freely in good growing conditions.

The youngest leaves are the most tender and flavourful, so cut plants back to encourage new growth if flavour diminishes over summer.

white or pink flowers are also available. **'Florescate'** produces pink-purple flowers. **'Grolau'** was developed for indoor use, has thicker leaves and a stronger flavour and produces best when cut freely. **'Staro'** is a hybrid with thicker leaves ideal for freezing. (Zones 3–8)

A. tuberosum (garlic chives) forms a clump of long, narrow, flat, dark green leaves. Clusters of white flowers are borne all summer. The young leaves have a distinctive garlic flavour. They are even more prone to self-seeding than chives. (Zones 3–8)

Problems and Pests
Chives rarely have any problems.

Chives are said to increase appetite and encourage good digestion.

Harvesting
Chives can be snipped off with scissors to use fresh all spring, summer and fall, and even winter if you grow them indoors, as needed.

Flowers are usually used just after they open, and the individual flowers in the cluster are broken apart for use in salads or sauces, or as garnish.

Tips
Chives are decorative enough to be included in a mixed or herbaceous border and can be left to naturalize. In an herb garden, chives should be given plenty of space to allow for self-seeding. Chives can also be grown in containers, even inside on the kitchen windowsill.

Recommended
A. schoenoprasum (chives) forms a clump of bright green, cylindrical leaves. Clusters of pinkish purple flowers are produced in early and midsummer. Varieties with

Dill

Anethum

Features: Clump-forming annual; feathery, edible foliage; yellow, summer flowers; edible seeds **Height:** 60 cm–1.5 m **Spread:** 30 cm or more

Dill is majestic and beautiful in any garden setting, and it is incredibly easy to grow, requiring only a little space. Its leaves and seeds are probably best known for their use as pickling herbs, though they have a wide variety of other culinary uses, providing a pleasant accompaniment to many dishes, cold and hot.

Starting
Dill can be sown directly into the garden around the last frost date. Make several small sowings every couple of weeks to ensure a steady supply of leaves.

Growing
Dill grows best in **full sun** in a **sheltered** location out of strong winds. The soil should be of **poor to average fertility, moist** and **well drained**.

Don't grow dill near fennel because the two plants will cross-pollinate, and the seeds of both plants will lose their distinct flavours.

Harvesting

Pick the leaves as needed throughout summer and dry them or freeze them for use in winter. Harvest the seeds by shaking the seed heads over a sheet once they ripen in late summer or fall.

Tips

With its feathery leaves, dill is an attractive addition to a mixed bed or border. It can be included in a vegetable garden but does well in any sunny location, including in a container on the balcony or patio, or even the kitchen windowsill.

Dill attracts butterflies and beneficial insects to the garden.

Recommended

A. graveolens forms a clump of feathery, aromatic foliage. Clusters of yellow flowers are borne at the tops of sturdy stems. **'Bouquet'** produces high seed and leaf yields. **'Fernleaf'** produces high yields of leaves in a dwarf form and is slow to bolt. **'Mammoth'** produces sparse foliage and quickly goes to seed, producing large seed heads. It is one of the best for pickling.

Problems and Pests

Dill rarely suffers from any problems.

Dill not only tastes delicious but also helps with the digestion of certain foods including cabbage, bread and cooked root vegetables.

Garlic

Allium

Features: edible, perennial bulb; narrow, strap-like leaves; white, summer flowers
Height: 15–60 cm **Spread:** 20 cm

Like most of its *Allium* relatives, garlic has a history of use thousands of years long. It is popular worldwide as a flavouring for food, and it is relatively easy to grow. So if you like to use it, go ahead and grow it.

Starting
Garlic is generally grown from sets (cloves) that can be started in fall or spring. Fall-planted garlic produces the largest bulbs at harvest time, but don't expect to see much development from this bulb until the following spring; all the fall growth will be underground, which gives the plant a head start in spring.

Plant cloves with the pointed end up and the root end down, skins intact, 5 cm deep and 15 cm apart.

Growing
Garlic grows best in **full sun**. The soil should be **fertile, moist** and **well drained**.

Recommended

A. sativum* var. *ophioscordon (hardneck garlic) has a stiff central stem around which the cloves develop. (Zones 3–8)

A. sativum* var. *sativum (softneck garlic) develops more cloves but has no stiff stem. The soft leaves are often used to braid garlic bulbs together for storage. It can be stored for a longer time than hardneck varieties. (Zones 3–8)

Problems and Pests

A few rot problems can occur, but this plant is generally trouble free.

In the garden, garlic works to repel several common garden pests.

Although the flowers are quite attractive and often intriguing, they should be removed so the plant devotes all its energy to bulb production rather than seed production.

Harvesting

This plant can be dug up in fall once the leaves have yellowed and died back. Lift gently with a garden fork to avoid cracking the bulbs. Allow the bulbs to dry completely before storing, and place them in a location with good air circulation.

Tips

Garlic is not the most ornamental plant, but it takes up very little space and can be tucked into any spare spot in your garden. It can also be grown in containers, provided they have enough depth.

Horseradish

Armoracia

Features: clump-forming perennial; glossy, green, creased leaves; pungent, edible root
Height: 60–90 cm **Spread:** 45 cm or more

Horseradish sauce is a popular condiment appreciated around the world for its unique pungent flavour. The horseradish plant, however, is too often relegated to a neglected back corner of the garden, despite its attractive foliage.

Starting
Plants can be purchased, or if you know someone with a horseradish plant, they can give you a division or a piece of root. As with dandelions, a new plant will generally grow from even a small piece of root. Plant dormant roots in early spring, 30 cm apart.

Growing
Horseradish grows well in **full sun**. The soil should be **light, moist, well drained** and of **average fertility**, but the plant adapts to most conditions.

Any roots left in the ground after fall harvest will produce new plants in spring. Left undisturbed, horseradish can become invasive. If it starts to get too big, simply dig it up and divide it into sections, replanting only what you want.

Harvesting

When the foliage dies back in fall, you can dig up some of the roots to use fresh or in preserves, relishes and pickles. The roots have the strongest flavour in fall, but they can be harvested at any time once the plant is well established.

Tips

Horseradish is a vigorous plant that spreads to form a sizeable clump. It is fairly adaptable and can be used in a somewhat neglected area, but it deserves a better spot because of its interesting foliage.

Because of its tendency to spread, horseradish is a good plant for a container, provided there is enough depth for the roots to develop.

Recommended

A. rusticana forms a large, spreading clump of large, puckered, dark green leaves. It has a large, white, tapered root with smaller offshoots. Plants grow up to 90 cm tall and spread 45 cm or more. The root can grow 60 cm deep. White flowers are produced in early to midsummer. **'Variegata'** produces variegated or marbled leaves with creamy markings. (Zones 3–8)

Problems and Pests

Generally problem free, horseradish can occasionally suffer from powdery mildew, downy mildew, fungal leaf spot or root rot.

Horseradish sauce is a popular garnish for roasted meats, roast beef in particular.

Mint

Mentha

Features: bushy, spreading perennial; fragrant foliage; purple, pink or white, summer flowers
Height: 15–90 cm **Spread:** 90 cm to indefinite

Indigenous to the Mediterranean area, mint was a favourite of the Romans, who brought it to all their occupied countries. It came to the Americas with the earliest settlers and promptly escaped into the wild. While used mostly for culinary purposes, mints have a long history of medicinal use for aiding digestion and calming upset stomachs.

Starting
Mint can be started from seed, but the seeds are unreliable; you may not end up with the mint you thought you were

getting. Instead, purchase the type of mint you want from a garden centre or nursery, or if you know someone with a desirable mint, ask for a cutting.

Growing
Mint grows well in **full sun** or **partial shade**. The soil should be **average to fertile, humus rich** and **moist**.

These plants spread vigorously by rhizomes and may need a barrier in the soil to restrict their spread. Cut them back frequently to keep them tidy and to encourage bushy growth.

M. spicata 'Crispa'

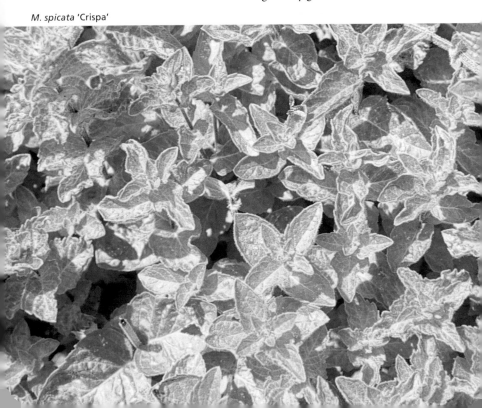

M. x piperita

Recommended

There are many species, hybrids and cultivars of mint. *M. x piperita* (peppermint) and *M. spicata* (spearmint) are two of the most commonly grown culinary varieties. There are also more decorative varieties with variegated or curly leaves, as well as varieties with unusual, fruit-scented leaves. '**Chocolate**' looks like a mint but tastes like chocolate. '**Margarita**' produces bold, lime-scented foliage. (Zones 3–8)

Problems and Pests

Problems with mildew, rust and leaf spot can occur.

Mint sauce and jelly are not just tasty condiments for lamb, but also, the volatile mint oils help to break down the meat fibres and stimulate the appetites of diners.

Harvesting

Harvest mint leaves at any time. They are best when used fresh, but they can be stored for a few days in a plastic bag in the refrigerator, or frozen in ice cube trays or dried for later use.

Tips

Mint makes a good groundcover and can be included in a border, though a root barrier might be needed to prevent excessive spread.

Mint is ideal in a container, both to prevent it from spreading and to keep it handy for use. Plus, you can bring it indoors over winter for fresh leaves year-round.

Bees, butterflies and other pollinators are attracted to the flowers of mint.

Oregano & Marjoram

Origanum

Features: bushy perennial; fragrant, edible foliage; white or pink, summer flowers
Height: 30–90 cm **Spread:** 20–45 cm

O. vulgare var. hirtum

Oregano and marjoram are two of the best known and most frequently used herbs. They are popular in stuffing, soups and stews, and no pizza is complete until it has been sprinkled with fresh or dried oregano.

Starting

These plants can be started from seed 4–6 weeks before you plan to plant them into the garden. You can also purchase plants, but use a reputable source so you can be sure you purchase the exact variety you want.

Growing

Oregano and marjoram grow best in **full sun**. The soil should be of **poor to average fertility, neutral to alkaline** and **well drained**. They are somewhat drought tolerant once established, and keeping them on the dry side concentrates flavour. New wood is most productive, so cut plants back in winter or spring. Oregano may self-seed.

Harvesting

Leaves can be picked as needed for fresh use or dried for later use. They retain much of their flavour when dried, especially if they are harvested just before the plants are in full flower.

Tips

These bushy perennials are herb garden staples. They make lovely additions to any border and can be trimmed to form low hedges. You can also try growing a pot of these herbs indoors for fresh use over winter; just be sure they have enough light.

Recommended

O. majorana (marjoram) is upright and shrubby. It has fuzzy, light green leaves and bears white or pink flowers in summer. Where it is not hardy, it can be grown as an annual. (Zones 7–9)

O. vulgare 'Aureum'

O. vulgare var. *hirtum* (oregano, Greek oregano) is the most flavourful culinary variety of oregano. This low, bushy plant has fuzzy, grey-green leaves and bears white flowers. Many other interesting varieties of *O. vulgare* are available, including some with golden, variegated or curly leaves. **'Aureum'** bears golden foliage with a mild flavour. **'Compactum'** has a mild flavour with a compact, dense growing habit. (Zones 5–9)

Problems and Pests

Problems with oregano and marjoram are rare.

The flowers attract pollinators and other beneficial insects to the garden.

Parsley

Petroselinum

Features: biennial grown as an annual; bushy habit; attractive, edible foliage
Height: 20–60 cm **Spread:** 30–60 cm

Parsley is far more than an attractive garnish. It is flavourful and full of vitamins, and it can brighten the flavour of just about any dish. Try both the curly-leaved and the flat-leaved varieties; each one has something to offer.

Starting
Parsley can be sown directly in the garden once the last frost date has passed, or 4–6 weeks earlier indoors. Start it in peat pots or in its permanent location because parsley resents having its roots disturbed.

Soaking the seeds for 24 hours improves germination.

Growing
Parsley grows well in **full sun** or **partial shade**. The soil should be **average to fertile, humus rich, moist** and **well drained**.

Pinch parsley back to encourage bushy growth. This plant can also be cut back regularly if you need a larger quantity in a recipe, and if not cut back too hard, it will sprout new growth.

Var. *neapolitanum*

that are desired and not the flowers or seeds. Cultivars may have flat or curly leaves. Flat leaves are tastier, and curly ones are more decorative. Dwarf cultivars are also available. **'Afro'** and **'Paramount'** produce tightly curled, dark green foliage. **'Clivi'** is a curly-leaved, dwarf cultivar. **Var. *neapolitanum*** produces flat leaves with stronger flavour.

Problems and Pests
Parsley rarely suffers from any problems.

A nutritious addition to a variety of dishes, parsley contains vitamins A and C as well as iron.

Harvesting
Cut sprigs as needed to use fresh throughout the growing season. Its flavour is best when used fresh, but it can also be dried. It maintains its green colour even after drying and will keep for months.

Tips
The bright green leaves and compact habit make parsley a good edging plant for beds and borders. It also grows well in containers, which can be kept close to the kitchen for easy picking and even brought indoors over winter for fresh parsley year-round.

Recommended
P. crispum forms a clump of bright green, divided leaves. This biennial is usually grown as an annual because it is the leaves

Rosemary

Rosmarinus

Features: tender, bushy or spreading, evergreen shrub; fragrant, edible foliage; bright blue, sometimes pink flowers **Height:** 20 cm–1.2 m **Spread:** 30 cm–1.2 m

The needle-like leaves of this fragrant little shrub are used to flavour a wide variety of foods, including chicken, pork, lamb, rice, tomato and egg dishes. A little fresh rosemary sprinkled on roasted vegetables is truly delicious. A Mediterranean native, this versatile herb performs well under a variety of conditions and has great value as a landscape plant.

Starting
Specific varieties of this plant can be purchased from garden centres, nurseries and specialty growers. Seed for the species is available but usually not for specific varieties. It can be started indoors in late winter.

Growing
Rosemary prefers **full sun** but tolerates partial shade. The soil should be of **poor to average fertility** and **well drained**. Rosemary takes well to frequent, light pruning.

Rosemary is not hardy in most of Canada. It is best to grow rosemary plants in containers, and treat them as houseplants during winter. Plants rarely reach their mature size when grown in containers.

To overwinter a tender container-grown plant, keep it in very light or partial shade outdoors in summer; then put it in a sunny window indoors for winter. Be careful not to overwater it; allow it to dry out slightly between waterings.

Harvesting
Leaves can be picked as needed for use in cooking.

Tips

Upright varieties of rosemary are best as a specimen in a container. Low-growing, spreading varieties can be grown in hanging baskets.

Recommended

R. officinalis is a dense, bushy, evergreen shrub with narrow, dark green leaves. The habit varies somewhat between cultivars, from strongly upright to prostrate and spreading. Flowers are usually shades of blue, but pink-flowered cultivars are available. Cultivars that are hardy in a sheltered spot in zone 6 with winter protection are also available. **'Arp'** is a particularly hardy variety. **'Blue Boy'** and **'Blue Spires'** are good varieties for indoor growing. **'Tuscan Blue'** is an upright, columnar selection with thick stems and succulent leaves, famous for its violet-blue flowers. (Zone 8)

Problems and Pests

Aphids and whiteflies can be a problem on plants overwintering indoors.

Rosemary attracts birds, butterflies and bees and repels carrot flies.

Sage

Salvia

Features: woody, mound-forming perennial; fragrant, decorative, edible foliage; blue or purple, summer flowers **Height:** 30–60 cm **Spread:** 45–90 cm

'Icterina'

Sage is perhaps best known as a flavouring for stuffing, but it has a great range of culinary uses, including in soups, stews, sausages and dumplings. It also has a long history of medicinal use.

Starting

Specific varieties of sage can be purchased, and the species can be started indoors in late winter or early spring.

Growing

Sage prefers **full sun** but tolerates light shade. The soil should be of **average fertility** and **well drained**. It tolerates drought once established.

This plant benefits from a light mulch of compost each year. A winter mulch of straw often provides enough protection for sage to survive up to a zone 3 winter.

'Tricolor'

available, including the silver-leaved **'Berggarten,'** the yellow-leaved **'Golden Sage,'** the yellow-margined **'Icterina,'** the purple-leaved **'Purpurea'** and the purple, green and cream variegated **'Tricolor,'** which also has a pink flush to the new growth. **'Compacta'** is a small version perfect for containers. (Zones 4–8)

Problems and Pests
Sage rarely suffers from any problems, but it can rot in wet soil.

Sage can be grown in a pot indoors, but it needs about a year to become established before it can be harvested. It might be best to reserve your indoor space for quicker-growing herbs.

Harvesting
Pick leaves as you need them for fresh use. They can be dried or frozen in late summer and fall for winter use.

Tips
Sage is a good plant for a border, adding volume to the middle or as an attractive edging or feature plant near the front. Sage can also be grown in mixed planters on the patio or balcony for convenient picking. Grown as a specimen in its own pot, it can be brought indoors over winter.

Recommended
S. officinalis (common sage) is a woody, mound-forming perennial with soft, grey-green leaves. Spikes of light purple or blue flowers appear in early and midsummer. Many cultivars with attractive foliage are

Savory

Satureja

Features: bushy annual or perennial; slender, erect stems; narrow, oblong leaves; small, white or pink, summer flowers **Height:** 30–40 cm **Spread:** 30 cm

Savory has a long history of culinary and medicinal uses, with the culinary being prominent in modern times. There are two main species: summer savory and winter savory. Both have their pros and cons, but both have a strong, spicy flavour that goes well with pork, poultry and fish, and also potato and bean dishes. Savory blends nicely with bay, sage and thyme.

Starting

Start savory indoors from seed approximately 4 weeks before the last frost in spring; plant seedlings once the danger of frost has passed.

Growing

Savory grows best in **full sun**. The soil should be of **poor to average fertility, neutral to alkaline** and **well drained**.

S. hortensis

Recommended

S. hortensis (summer savory) is a bushy, aromatic annual with narrow leaves. It bears white or pink flowers in summer. The species grows 30 cm tall with an equal spread. '**Aromata**' is a compact form with higher oil content in its leaves. '**Midget**' is a bushier, taller selection with high essential oil content.

S. montana (winter savory) is a bushy, semi-evergreen perennial. Its narrow, dark green leaves stay on the plant through early winter and are strong and pungent. It bears white, summer flowers and grows 30–40 cm tall, with a 30 cm spread. '**Nana**' is a dwarf cultivar. (Zones 5–9)

Problems and Pests

Savory rarely suffers from any problems.

In colder areas, winter savory will go dormant in winter but will come back in spring. Divide it every 2 years to keep good flavour.

Harvesting

Pick leaves as needed for fresh use; new growth tastes the best. If a large amount is needed, cut up to 20 cm off the top of the plant.

Tips

Savory is attractive in the front of beds and borders. It doesn't like too much moisture, so it is better suited to a rock garden than a vegetable garden. Try it in an herb garden with other plants that like similar conditions.

It can also be grown in a container, with the bonus that you won't have to water it every day. It can be brought indoors over winter.

Summer savory is a principle ingredient in the famous French herb mixture herbs de Provence.

Winter savory loses much of its flavour with prolonged cooking.

S. montana

Tarragon

Artemisia

Features: bushy perennial; narrow, fragrant, edible leaves; airy flowers
Height: 45–90 cm **Spread:** 30–60 cm

It's ironic that this plant gets as large as it does because you need only a tiny amount to flavour a dish. The distinctive licorice-like flavour of tarragon lends itself to a wide variety of meat and vegetable dishes and is the key flavouring in Bernaise sauce. It is also one of the four *fines herbes* used in French cooking.

Starting
The tastiest tarragon is French tarragon, and it can be propagated only vegetatively. Seeds do not come true to type. Plants can be purchased at nurseries and garden centres and from specialty growers. Plant them out once the risk of frost has passed.

Growing
Tarragon grows best in **full sun** but tolerates partial shade. The soil should be **average to fertile, moist** and **well drained**.

Tarragon benefits from heavy mulching during the winter months to protect the roots. Divide the plant every few years in spring to keep it vigorous and to encourage the best leaf flavour.

Harvesting

Pick leaves as needed to use fresh, and dry or freeze some in late summer for winter use.

Tips

Tarragon is not exceptionally decorative, but it does provide a good vertical presence. It can be included in a herb garden or mixed border, where the surrounding plants will support its tall stems. It will also do well on its own in a container, outside or on the kitchen windowsill.

Recommended

A. dracunculus* var. *sativa (French tarragon) is a bushy, clump-forming perennial with tall stems and narrow, aromatic, tender leaves. Airy clusters of insignificant, pale yellow flowers are produced in late summer. (Zones 3–8)

Problems and Pests

Tarragon rarely suffers from any problems.

Before purchasing a plant, chew a leaf to see if it has the distinct flavour it should have. French tarragon is preferred; Russian tarragon (A. d. var. dracunculoides) is a more vigorous plant but has little of the desired flavour.

Thyme

Thymus

Features: bushy perennial; fragrant, decorative, edible foliage; purple, pink or white, summer flowers **Height:** 20–45 cm **Spread:** 20–60 cm

Thyme is a popular culinary herb used in soups, stews, casseroles and roasts. It also has many medicinal uses. All thyme species are rich in volatile oils; place your thyme where passersby can brush against it to release the pleasant fragrance.

Starting

Common thyme can be started indoors from seed 4–6 weeks before you plan to plant it outdoors. This plant can also be purchased at nurseries and garden centres and from specialty growers.

Growing

Thyme prefers **full sun**. The soil should be **neutral to alkaline,** of **poor to average fertility** and very **well drained**. Good drainage is essential. It is beneficial to work leaf mould and sharp limestone gravel into the soil to improve structure and drainage. Thyme is drought tolerant once established.

Once the plant has finished flowering, shear it back by about half to encourage new growth and to prevent it from becoming too woody.

T. x citriodorus 'Argenteus'

Harvesting

Pick leaves as needed for fresh use or to dry for later use.

Tips

Thyme is useful for sunny, dry locations at the front of borders, between or beside paving stones, on rock walls and in containers such as window boxes and hanging baskets. It can be grown indoors for fresh use over winter, provided it has enough light.

Recommended

T. x citriodorus (lemon thyme) forms a mound of lemon-scented, dark green foliage. The summer flowers are pale pink. Cultivars with silver- or gold-margined leaves are available. **'Archer's Gold'** is a compact plant with bright yellow, lemony foliage and pale purple flowers. (Zones 4–9)

T. vulgaris (common thyme) forms a bushy mound of fragrant, dark green leaves. The summer flowers may be purple, pink or white. Cultivars with variegated leaves are available. **'Silver Posie'** is the best of the silver thyme selections, bearing white variegated leaves and pale purple-pink flowers. (Zones 3–8)

Problems and Pests

Thyme rarely suffers from any problems, but its roots can rot in poorly drained, wet soils.

Thyme is a bee magnet when it is blooming. Pleasant herbal thyme honey goes well with biscuits.

Amaranth

Amaranthus

Features: bushy, upright annual; red, purple, burgundy, gold or green, plume-like flower clusters; edible young growth and seeds **Height:** 1.2–2.7 m **Spread:** 30–90 cm

Amaranth is most commonly known to gardeners as an ornamental, but it provides one of the most complete sources of protein available in a seed. It is prolific, producing up to 10,000 seeds in a single flower head. Not only are the seeds nutritious and delicious, but so too are the leaves, stems and young shoots.

Starting

Amaranth sprouts quickly when sown directly in the garden. Scatter seeds or plant in rows once all danger of frost has passed and the soil has warmed—mid-May to early June for most Canadian gardens.

Growing

Amaranth grows best in **full sun**. It adapts to most soil conditions, but it prefers a **fertile** soil. Spread a layer of compost on the soil before you plant to keep weeds down and to improve the soil. Although it tolerates drought, this plant grows best if the soil is kept fairly moist while it germinates.

Harvesting

The seeds usually ripen and fall about the time of the first fall frost. Over a drop cloth, large bowl or bucket, shake or rub the seed heads between your hands—wear gloves because the seed heads are quite coarse. The seeds and plant bits are easy to separate because the plant bits are lighter and rise to the surface if you run your hands through the collected seeds and carefully blow a fan over them. The seeds are quite light, too, so make sure the breeze is not too strong. Leave the seeds

'**Plainsman**' is a compact selection bearing burgundy seed heads followed by heaps of purple seeds.

Four species of amaranth are grown for their edible leaves: **A. blitum, A. cruentus, A. dubius** and **A. tricolor**. The edible leaf species are similar in appearance and form. Many selections are available.

Problems and Pests

Young plants look similar to red-rooted pigweed, making weeding challenging. If red-rooted pigweed is common in your garden, start your amaranth plants in peat pots, then transplant them directly into the garden to make weed identification easier.

to dry in a warm place before storing them in an airtight container.

The leaves can be harvested at any point throughout the season and used as you would spinach.

Tips

This plant is very tall and makes a good screen plant. It resembles giant celosia when in bloom and is indeed related to that popular annual. The flowers can be used in fresh or dried arrangements, but cutting the flowers will reduce your seed yield.

Recommended

Three species of amaranth are grown for their seeds: **A. caudatus, A. cruentus** and **A. hypochondriacus**. These species are tall, annual plants that produce large, plume-like clusters of red, purple, gold or green flowers. Several cultivars are available, including '**Burgundy**,' with purple-red leaves and large burgundy plumes; '**Golden Giant**,' with bright yellow stems and flowers that mature to deep gold; and '**Mercado**,' with dense, less plume-like, bright green flower heads. '**Popping**' produces seeds suitable for popping, and

The seeds can be added to soups and stews, cooked as a hot cereal or side dish, or ground into flour and used in pancakes, muffins and breads. They can even be popped, like corn, for snacking.

A. caudatus

Caraway

Carum

Features: hardy biennial; feathery, light green, edible foliage; clusters of tiny, white flowers; edible seeds **Height:** 20–60 cm **Spread:** 30 cm

In use for over 5000 years, caraway is a tasty addition to savoury and sweet dishes. The seeds are used in sauerkraut, stews, rye bread, pies and coleslaw. The feathery leaves can be used fresh in salads, stews and vegetable stir-fries. Having caraway in your garden or in a pot on your windowsill will open up new taste sensations in your daily cooking.

Starting

Caraway can be started from seed and should be planted where you want it to grow because it can bolt (go to flower) quickly when the roots are disturbed.

Growing

Caraway grows best in **full sun** but tolerates some shade. The soil should be **fertile, loose** and **well drained**.

This plant is biennial and generally doesn't bloom until the second year. It is a vigorous self-seeder.

Caraway is dependably hardy to zone 5. In colder gardens, it will benefit from a good mulch in fall.

Harvesting

Pick leaves as needed to use fresh.

The seeds are the most commonly used part of the plant. The seed heads are ripe when the seed pods just begin to open and the seeds turn brown. Cut the ripe seed heads from the plants, and place them in a paper bag. Loosely tie the bag closed, and hang it in a warm, dry location. Once the seeds are dry, they can be stored in an airtight jar.

Tips

Caraway doesn't have a very strong presence in the garden, but it can be planted in groups with more decorative plants where its ferny foliage and pretty white flowers add a delicate, airy touch. It will also do well on its own in a container, provided there is enough depth to accommodate its taproot.

Recommended

C. carvi is a delicate-looking, upright biennial with ferny foliage. In the second summer after sowing, white flowers are borne in flat-topped clusters above the foliage. Ridged fruits or seeds follow after the flowers. (Zones 3–9)

Problems and Pests

Caraway rarely suffers from any pests or problems.

Planting caraway near your cabbages will attract beneficial predatory insects and will also help you to remember to add some caraway seed to your cabbage as it cooks. Caraway helps to reduce the cooking odour and the flatulence that can be a by-product of eating cabbage.

Coriander • Cilantro

Coriandrum

Features: upright, clump-forming annual; lacy, edible foliage; clusters of tiny, white flowers; edible seeds **Height:** 45–60 cm **Spread:** 20–45 cm

Coriander is a multi-purpose herb. The leaves, called cilantro, are used in salads, salsas and soups. The seeds, called coriander, are used in cakes, pies, chutneys and marmalades. The flavour of each is quite distinct.

Starting

Coriander can be started from seed 4–6 weeks before the last frost date or sown directly in the garden. Started plants can also be purchased from nurseries, garden centres or herb specialists. Several small sowings 2 weeks apart will ensure a steady supply of leaves.

Growing

Coriander prefers **full sun** but benefits from afternoon shade during the heat of summer in hotter parts of Canada. The soil should be **fertile, light** and **well drained**. This plant dislikes humid conditions and does best during a dry summer.

Harvesting

Leaves can be harvested as needed throughout summer. The lower, older leaves have the strongest flavour.

Seeds can be harvested as they ripen in fall; watch for them to turn brown. Spread out a large sheet and shake the seed heads over it to collect the seeds. Dry the seeds and then store them in an airtight container.

Tips

Coriander is a delight to behold when in flower, but it has pungent leaves and is best planted where people who don't appreciate the scent won't have to brush past it. Add a plant here and there throughout your borders.

If you do like the scent, keep it in a pot on your patio or balcony for easy access to the

cilantro. You can even grow it indoors on the kitchen windowsill.

Recommended

C. sativum is an annual herb that forms a clump of lacy basal foliage, above which large, loose clusters of tiny, white flowers are produced. The seeds ripen in late summer and fall. **'Cilantro'** produces flavourful foliage. **'Morocco'** is a fine selection for seed production.

Problems and Pests

This plant rarely suffers from any problems.

Coriander is one of the best plants for attracting beneficial predatory insects to your garden, but do not plant coriander near dill or fennel; cross-pollination reduces seed production and makes the seed flavour of each one less distinct.

Fennel

Foeniculum

Features: upright, short-lived perennial; attractive, fragrant, feathery foliage; yellow, late summer flowers; edible seeds **Height:** 60 cm–1.8 m **Spread:** 30–60 cm

Fennel has been used for thousands of years in one capacity or another. Herbalists have touted its healing capabilities, and cooks have used fennel as both a vegetable and a herb in a variety of ways. This plant even possesses cosmetic qualities and is said to smooth wrinkles and lines on the face as well as refresh tired eyes.

Starting

Seeds can be started directly in the garden around the last frost date or about 4 weeks earlier indoors.

Growing

Fennel grows best in **full sun**. The soil should be **average to fertile, moist** and **well drained**.

Avoid planting fennel near dill or coriander because cross-pollination reduces seed production and makes the seed flavour of each less distinct. Fennel easily self-sows.

Harvesting

Harvest fennel leaves as needed for fresh use.

Var. *azoricum*

The seeds can be harvested when ripe, in late summer or fall. Shake the seed heads over a sheet to collect the seeds. Let them dry out before storing them.

Florence fennel can be harvested as soon as the bulbous base becomes swollen. Pull plants up as needed, and harvest any left in the ground at the end of the season before the first fall frost.

Tips

Fennel is an attractive addition to a mixed bed or border. The flowers attract pollinators and beneficial predatory insects to the garden. Fennel will also do well on its own in a container.

Recommended

F. vulgare is a short-lived perennial that forms clumps of loose, feathery foliage. It grows 60 cm–1.8 m tall and spreads 30–60 cm. Clusters of small, yellow flowers are borne in late summer. The seeds ripen in fall. The species is primarily grown for its seeds and leaves. **Var. *azoricum*** (Florence fennel, finocchio) is a biennial that forms a large, edible bulb at the stem base.

This variety is grown for its stem, leaves and licorice-flavoured bulb. '**Solaris**' is a large, uniform selection, producing semi-flat bulbs that are vigorous and resistant to bolting. '**Zefa Fino**' is ready for harvest in 80 days, bolt resistant and very large. It bears flattish bulbs, green almost to the root. '**Orion**' is also ready in 80 days and has large, thick, rounded bulbs. It has a higher yield than open-pollinated varieties, a nice anise flavour and a crisp texture. **Var. *dulce*** (sweet fennel) bears green-brown seeds. '**Purpureum**' ('Atropurpureum'; bronze fennel) is similar in appearance to the species but has bronzy purple foliage. This cultivar is usually sold as an ornamental, but all parts are entirely edible.

Problems and Pests

Fennel rarely suffers from any problems.

Fennel bulbs combine well with many other vegetables in savoury recipes but make an interesting addition to sweet recipes, too. Try adding some to your next fruit salad.

Flax

Linum

Features: upright annual; blue flowers; edible seeds
Height: 30–90 cm Spread: 20–45 cm

Flaxseed has long been added to baked muffins, breads and cereals. It is now being hailed for its fantastic health-improving potential and is an excellent source of omega-3 fatty acids. Both brown and golden seeds have identical nutrition profiles and the same number of omega-3 fatty acids.

Starting
Start seed directly in the garden around the last frost date.

Growing
Flax grows best in **full sun**. The soil should be of **average fertility, light, humus rich** and **well drained**. Although

flax often ceases blooming during the warmest part of summer, it generally begins again when the weather cools in late summer and fall.

Harvesting

When they are ripe, harvest the seeds by rubbing the seed heads between your hands over a sheet or bucket. Dry the seeds completely before storing them in a cool, dry place.

Tips

Flax is a beautiful plant that many gardeners grow for its ornamental appeal alone. If seeds are wanted, you are going to need a fair number of plants, but as they are so attractive, a mass planting should not be a problem.

Recommended

L. usitatissimum is a clump-forming annual with leafy, upright stems that wave in the slightest breeze. Each of the blue, summer flowers lasts only one day and is replaced by another every day once blooming begins. The flowers are followed by chestnut brown, pale brown or golden yellow seeds in late summer or fall.

Problems and Pests

Problems with rot, rust, wilt, slugs, snails and aphids can occur.

This species is not used exclusively as a food source; the stems of some cultivars are processed to produce linen. Linseed oil also comes from the seeds of flax.

Poppy

Papaver

Features: basal annual; hairy stems and leaves; red, pink, white or purple, single or double flowers; edible seeds **Height:** 30 cm–1.2 m **Spread:** 20–45 cm

Poppy seeds are a frequent addition to baked goods, and poppy seed oil has many uses as well. Although opiates are derived from these poppies, the seeds contain only low levels. Remarkably easy to grow, poppies add abundant colour to your garden.

Starting

Direct sow poppies in spring. Several successive smaller sowings will give you a longer flower display, but this isn't necessary if you are just growing poppies for the seeds. The seeds are very small, and you will get better distribution if you mix them with fine sand before you plant them. Do not cover the seeds because they need light to germinate.

Growing

Poppies grow best in **full sun**. The soil should be **fertile, sandy, humus rich** and **well drained**. Good drainage is essential.

Poppies self-seed freely and are likely to continue to spring up randomly in your garden once you've planted them.

Harvesting

You will know the seeds are ready to be harvested when the pods begin to dry and you can hear the seeds rattle in the pods when you shake them gently. Cut the heads off, turn them upside down and shake the seeds into a paper bag. Let them dry in the paper bag and then store the seeds in a jar or other container.

Tips

Poppies work well in mixed borders where other plants are slow to fill in. Poppies will fill empty spaces early in the season then die back over summer, leaving room for other plants.

Poppies are also a good option for a container, especially if you like to change up your container plantings frequently.

Recommended

P. somniferum (opium poppy) forms a basal rosette of foliage above which leafy stems bear red, pink, white or purple flowers. Large, blue-green seed pods follow the

flowers. Propagation of the species is restricted in many countries because of its narcotic properties. Several acceptable cultivars are available for ornamental and culinary purposes. Blue-, white- or brown-seeded varieties are available.

Problems and Pests

Poppies rarely suffer from any problems.

Even though this is, indeed, the same plant that is used to produce heroin, growing it in Canada is unlikely to give you any trouble with law enforcement. Poppies need intense, prolonged heat to develop enough of the compounds necessary to produce any quantity of extractable narcotics, and we just don't get that kind of weather in Canada.

'Hens and Chickens'

Quinoa

Chenopodium

Features: branching, upright annual; soft leaves; attractive flower heads; good fall colour; edible seeds **Height:** 1.5–2.4 m **Spread:** 30–45 cm

Quinoa is a good choice for Canadian gardens; it grows well in our climate and enjoys our summer temperatures, and it looks great in the garden. The colourful seed heads form in clusters at the tips of the branches. The protein-rich, nutty-flavoured seeds are the reward at the end of the season.

Starting

Sow directly in the garden once the soil has dried out a bit and can be worked. Young plants can tolerate a light frost. Seeds can be scattered over an area or planted in rows. Keep the seedbed moist during germination. Thin the seedlings to 30–45 cm apart.

Growing

Quinoa grows best in **full sun**. The soil should be **average to fertile** and **well drained,** though the plant adapts to most conditions and tolerates drought once established. A layer of mulch will conserve moisture and keep weeds down, though quinoa's leafy habit tends to suppress weed growth once the plants start to fill in.

Harvesting

The seeds generally ripen around the time of the first fall frost. The leaves die back around the same time, making harvesting a simple matter of grasping the stem with a gloved hand and pulling upward to

that produce plenty of yellow seeds. **'Multi-hued'** bears flowers in shades of red, orange and purple. **'Temuco'** has chartreuse and red seed heads and white seeds.

Problems and Pests

Leaves are eaten by a few insects and are susceptible to a few diseases, but seed production is rarely affected.

Quinoa seeds are coated in a bitter substance called saponin. Lighter coloured seeds have less saponin. Rinse the seeds in water to wash the saponin off; the water will cease to foam when the saponin is gone. You can even put the seeds in a pillowcase or mesh bag and run them through a cycle in the washing machine (without soap) to rinse large quantities thoroughly.

remove the seeds. Remove plant bits by running your hands through the collected seeds on a slightly breezy day or by blowing a fan across the surface to blow away the dry plant bits. Seeds should be dried completely before storing.

Tips

This lovely, tall plant, with its seed heads that ripen to shades of gold, orange and red, is a welcome addition to the fall garden. Combine it with other tall fall bloomers, such as sunflowers and amaranth, to create a stunning display along a fence or wall.

Recommended

C. quinoa is a tall, leafy, branching annual. Flowers are borne in dense clusters along the tips of the stems. The leaves turn shades of orange and red in fall, and the seed heads ripen to shades of red, orange, gold, green or pink. Seeds may be brown, yellow or white. There are many cultivars, though they can be a bit difficult to find. **'Isluga'** has yellow-gold or pink seed heads

Sunflower

Helianthus

Features: tall, upright annual; daisy-like, yellow, orange, red, brown, cream or bicoloured flowers, typically with brown, purple or rusty red centres; edible seeds
Height: 90 cm–2.7 m **Spread:** 30 cm–1.2 m

Sunflowers make wonderful companions for other tall seed-bearing plants such as amaranth and quinoa. Sunflower seeds are popular as snacks and in cooking and baking, and sunflower seed butter is becoming a popular substitute for peanut butter.

Starting
Sunflowers can be sown directly into the garden in spring around the last frost date. Water well until the plants become established.

Growing
Sunflowers grow best in **full sun**. The soil should be of **average fertility, humus rich, moist** and **well drained**, though plants adapt to a variety of conditions. They become quite drought tolerant as summer progresses. These tall plants may need staking in windy or exposed locations.

Harvesting

Sunflower seeds are ready to harvest when the flower has withered and the seeds are plump. You may need to cover the flower heads with a paper bag or net to prevent birds from eating all the seeds before you get to them.

Tips

Sunflowers make a striking addition to the back of the border and along fences and walls. Dwarf selections can be grown in containers on the deck or balcony.

Recommended

H. annuus can develop a single stem or many branches. The large-flowered sunflowers usually develop a single stem. Many of the ornamental sunflowers offered in gardening catalogues have edible seeds. '**Russian Mammoth**,' a tall cultivar with large, yellow flowers, is one of the most popular for seed production. Several dwarf cultivars are also available.

Problems and Pests

Plants are generally problem free, but keeping birds away from the seeds until they are ready to be picked can be troublesome.

Sunflowers are a great way to invite birds into your garden if you don't mind not having the seeds for yourself. The birds will feast on garden pests as well as the seeds the flowers provide.

Beebalm

Bergamot

Monarda

Features: bushy perennial; fragrant, edible leaves; red or pink, edible, summer flowers
Height: 60 cm–1.2 m **Spread:** 30–60 cm

Beebalm is a member of the huge and widespread mint family and has both culinary and medicinal uses. The fresh leaves can be added to salads, and the fresh or dried leaves may be used to make a refreshing, minty, citrus-scented tea. The flowers make a decorative garnish for salads and desserts.

Starting

Sow seeds indoors in mid-spring, and plant out seedlings in early summer. Beebalm can also be started from cuttings.

Growing

Beebalm grows well in **full sun, partial shade** or **light shade**. The soil should be of **average fertility, humus rich, moist** and

Recommended
M. didyma is a bushy, mounding plant that forms a thick clump of stems with red or pink, summer flowers. '**Gardenview Scarlet**' bears large, scarlet flowers and is less susceptible to powdery mildew. '**Jacob Cline**' is taller and should be cut back by half in June to prevent flopping. It bears enormous, bight red flowers and is resistant to powdery mildew. '**Marshall's Delight**' doesn't come true to type from seed; it must be propagated by cuttings or divisions. It bears pink flowers and is resistant to powdery mildew. '**Panorama**' is a group of hybrids with flowers in scarlet, pink or salmon. (Zones 3–8)

Problems and Pests
Powdery mildew is the worst problem, but rust, leaf spot and leaf hoppers can also cause trouble. Do not allow the plant to dry out for extended periods.

*The alternative name, bergamot, comes from the similarity of this plant's scent to that of bergamot orange (*Citrus bergamia*), which is used in aromatherapy and to flavour Earl Grey tea.*

well drained. It will spread in moist, fertile soils, but the roots are close to the surface and can be removed easily.

In June, cut back some of the stems by half to extend the flowering period and to encourage compact growth. Thinning the stems also helps prevent powdery mildew. If mildew strikes after flowering, cut the plants back to 15 cm to increase air circulation. Divide every 2 or 3 years in spring just as new growth emerges.

Harvesting
Pick leaves and flowers as needed to use fresh, or dry them for later use.

Tips
Use beebalm beside a stream or pond or in a lightly shaded, well-watered border to attract bees, butterflies and hummingbirds to your garden. It can be grown in a container, provided it is kept sufficiently moist.

Borage

Borago

Features: bushy, bristly annual; edible, bristly leaves; edible, blue, purple or white, summer flowers **Height:** 45–60 cm **Spread:** 30–45 cm

Both leaves and flowers of borage are edible, making an interesting addition to salads. They have a light, cucumber-like flavour. The pretty flowers can also be frozen in ice cubes as decoration for summer drinks, or candied and used to decorate cakes and other desserts.

Starting

Seed can be sown directly in the garden in spring. This plant resents being transplanted because it has long taproots, but it recovers fairly quickly if moved when young.

Growing

Borage grows well in **full sun** or **partial shade**. The soil should be of **average fertility, light** and **well drained**, but this plant adapts to most conditions. It makes a good choice in a dry location because it doesn't require much water to thrive.

The plant should be pinched back when it is young to encourage bushy growth;

otherwise, it tends to flop over and develop a sprawling habit.

Borage is a vigorous self-seeder. Once you have established it in your garden, you will never have to plant it again. Young seedlings can be pulled up if they are growing where you don't want them.

Harvesting

Pick borage leaves when they are young and fuzzy—they become rather bristly as they mature. Flowers can be picked any time after they open; they tend to change colour from blue to pinkish mauve as they mature.

Tips

Borage makes an attractive addition to herb and vegetable gardens, as well as to flower beds and borders. Borage is also a good plant for mixed containers, including window boxes and hanging baskets.

Recommended

B. officinalis is a bushy plant with bristly leaves and stems. It bears clusters of star-shaped, blue or purple flowers from mid-summer to fall. A white-flowered variety is available.

Problems and Pests

Rare outbreaks of powdery mildew and aphids are possible but don't seem to be detrimental to the plant.

Borage attracts bees, butterflies and other pollinators, as well as other beneficial insects to the garden.

Calendula
Pot Marigold, English Marigold
Calendula

Features: hardy annual; yellow, orange, cream, gold or apricot, edible flowers; long blooming period **Height:** 25–60 cm **Spread:** 20–50 cm

'Apricot Surprise'

Bright and charming, calendula produces attractive, colourful flowers in summer and fall. Calendula flowers are popular kitchen herbs that can be added to stews and salads for colour and flavour.

Starting
Calendula grows easily from seed. Sprinkle the seeds where you want them to grow (they don't like to be transplanted), and cover them lightly with soil. They will sprout within a week.

Young plants are often difficult to find in nurseries because this plant is so quick and easy to start from seed.

Growing
Calendula does equally well in **full sun** or **partial shade**. The soil should be of **average fertility** and **well drained**. Calendula

'Apricot Surprise'

in shades of yellow, orange and apricot. **'Pacific Beauty'** is an heirloom cultivar with large, brightly coloured flowers. It grows 45–60 cm tall. **'Indian Prince'** bears large, double, burnt orange flowers with mahogany centres on plants that grow 60 cm tall.

Problems and Pests

Calendula is usually trouble free. It continues to perform well even when afflicted with rare problems such as aphids, whiteflies, smut, powdery mildew and fungal leaf spot.

Dried calendula flowers can be used as a saffron substitute for colouring food.

likes cool weather and can withstand a moderate frost.

Deadhead the plant to prolong blooming and keep it looking neat. If your plant fades in the summer heat, cut it back to 10–15 cm to encourage new growth. A fading plant can also be pulled up and new seeds planted. Both methods provide a good fall display.

Harvesting

Flowers can be picked as needed for fresh use, or the petals can be dried for later use.

Tips

This informal plant looks attractive in borders and mixed in among vegetables or other plants. It can also be used in mixed planters and container gardens.

Calendula is a cold-hardy annual and often continues flowering, even through a layer of snow, until the ground freezes completely.

Recommended

C. officinalis is a vigorous, tough, upright plant that grows 30–60 cm tall and spreads 25–50 cm. It bears single or double, daisy-like flowers in a wide range of yellow and orange shades. **'Bon Bon'** is a dwarf plant that grows 25–30 cm tall and bears flowers

Chamomile

Chamaemelum, Matricaria

Features: bushy annual or perennial; fragrant, feathery foliage; daisy-like, edible flowers
Height: 15–60 cm **Spread:** 15–45 cm

Chamomile's pretty, flavourful flowers can be used to make a perfect after-dinner tea. This delicate, airy plant is useful for filling in garden spaces wherever it is planted. The flowers can also be dried and stored so that you can enjoy chamomile tea through the winter months.

C. nobile

Starting

Seeds can be started about 4 weeks early indoors or sown directly in the garden once the last frost date has passed.

Growing

Chamomile grows best in **full sun**. The soil should be of **average fertility, sandy** and **well drained**.

M. recutita

welcome on a patio or balcony when grown in a container.

The flowers attract beneficial insects, so you may also want to plant a few here and there among your other plants.

Recommended

C. nobile (Roman chamomile) is a low-growing perennial that forms a mat of feathery foliage. It bears tiny, daisy-like flowers in summer. It grows 15–30 cm tall and spreads about 45 cm. (Zones 4–8)

M. recutita (German chamomile) is an upright annual with soft, finely divided, fern-like foliage and bears small, daisy-like flowers in summer. It grows 30–60 cm tall and spreads 15–20 cm.

Problems and Pests

Chamomile rarely suffers from any problems.

To prevent damping off, make a strong tea from ¼ cup of chamomile blossoms and 2 cups of boiling water. Let it steep overnight, then strain it and pour the tea into a spray bottle. Spray seedlings and seed-starting medium regularly.

Chamomile self-seeds freely if you don't pick all the flowers. Roman chamomile can be divided to maintain its vigour, but it is often simpler to pull up faded plants and let new ones fill in.

Harvesting

As the flowers mature, the petals fall off and the centres swell as the seeds start to develop. At this point, the flowers can be picked and used fresh or dried for tea.

Tips

Chamomile is an attractive plant to use along the edge of a pathway or to edge beds where the fragrance will be released when the foliage is brushed against, bruised or crushed. Its scent is also

Marigold

Tagetes

Features: upright annual; fragrant foliage; yellow, red, orange, brown, gold, cream or bicoloured, edible flowers **Height:** 15–90 cm **Spread:** 15–60 cm

T. lemmonii

From the large, exotic, ruffled flowers of African marigold to the tiny flowers of the low-growing signet marigold, the warm colours and fresh scent of these plants add a festive touch to the garden. The flowers are a tasty treat; they have a citrus-like flavour.

Starting

Marigolds can be started early indoors or sown directly in the garden around the last frost date. Plants can also be purchased from garden centres and nurseries.

Growing

Marigolds grow best in **full sun**. The soil should be of **average fertility** and **well drained**. These plants are drought tolerant but also hold up well in windy, rainy weather. Deadhead to prolong blooming and to keep plants tidy.

Harvesting

Flowers should be picked for use once they are fully open and used fresh. They tend to lose their colour and flavour when dried and don't freeze well. Remove the outer petals and bitter centre.

Leaves of signet, lemon mint and Mexican mint marigolds can be picked as needed for use in teas, soups and salads.

Tips

Dot these plants in small groups throughout your beds and borders for a pretty display, as well as to take advantage of their reputed nematode-repelling properties. Marigolds also make lovely additions to sunny container plantings.

Recommended

Although *T. erecta* (Aztec marigold, African marigold), *T. patula* (French marigold) and their hybrids have edible

T. tenuifolia

flowers, *T. lemmonii* (lemon mint marigold), *T. lucida* (Mexican mint marigold, Texas tarragon) and *T. tenuifolia* (signet marigold) are the most common culinary species. **Pumila Series** is a dwarf group bearing finely fringed leaves and lemony scented flowers.

Problems and Pests

Slugs and snails can ravage the foliage of all marigolds.

The Aztecs revered marigolds and used them in religious ceremonies.

Nasturtium

Tropaeolum

Features: bushy or trailing annual; attractive, edible foliage; red, orange, yellow, burgundy, pink, cream, gold, white or bicoloured, edible flowers **Height:** 30–45 cm for dwarf varieties; up to 3 m for trailing varieties **Spread:** equal to height

These fast-growing, brightly coloured flowers are easy to grow, making them popular with beginners and experienced gardeners alike. The edible leaves and flowers add a peppery flavour and visual interest to salads.

Starting
Direct sow seed once the danger of frost has passed. If you start them early indoors, sow them in individual peat pots to avoid disturbing the roots during transplanting.

Growing
Nasturtiums prefer **full sun** but tolerate some shade. The soil should be of **poor to average fertility, light, moist** and **well drained**. Soil that is too rich or has too much fertilizer results in a lot of leaves and very few flowers. Let the soil drain completely between waterings.

Harvesting
Pick leaves and flowers for fresh use as needed.

'Dwarf Jewel Mix'

Tips

Nasturtiums are used in beds, borders, containers and hanging baskets and on sloped banks. The climbing varieties are grown up trellises and over rock walls or places that need concealing. These plants thrive in poor locations, and they make interesting additions to plantings on hard-to-mow slopes.

Recommended

T. majus has a trailing habit, but many of the cultivars have bushier, more refined habits. Cultivars offer differing flower colours or variegated foliage. **Alaska Series** plants have white-marbled foliage. **Jewel Series** plants are compact, growing 30 cm tall and wide, with double flowers in a mix of deep orange, red or gold. **'Peach Melba'** forms a 30 cm mound. The flowers are pale yellow with a bright orange-red splash at the base of each petal. **'Whirlybird'** is a compact, bushy plant. The single or double flowers in shades of red, pink, yellow or orange do not have spurs.

Problems and Pests

These plants rarely suffer from any problems.

Use the flowers to make nasturtium butter. Finely chop the flowers and mix them into softened, unsalted butter; shape into a log and refrigerate. The butter will have a delicious zing and a delightful, confetti-like appearance.

Pansy & Violet

Viola

Features: low annual or perennial; edible, attractive, dark green foliage; edible, fragrant flowers
Height: 10–25 cm **Spread:** 15–30 cm

V. tricolor

Pansies and violets are some of the most popular flowers, and it's no wonder; they're beautiful and easy to grow, and as a bonus, they're edible. The leaves are hot and spicy and taste great in a salad, and the flowers have a mild wintergreen flavour, also great for salads or for decorating desserts.

Starting
Start seeds or purchase plants from the garden centre in spring.

Growing
Violets and pansies grow well in **partial shade** or **light shade**. The soil should be **fertile, humus rich, moist** and **well drained**.

Pinch off spent violet blooms and fertilize only once after blooming. Violets self-seed freely, so leave some flowers in place if more plants are desired.

Annual pansies will thrive in spring and fall, but may wilt in midsummer heat.

Simply trim them back, give them some fertilizer, keep the soil moist and wait for them to bloom again when the weather cools.

Harvesting

Pick flowers and leaves to use fresh as needed, or pick lots of flowers to dry and candy.

Tips

Pansies and violets work well in the ground in a woodland setting, or in mixed containers—just don't plant them with anything too aggressive. They look cheery in window boxes.

Recommended

V. odorata (fragrant violet, sweet violet) is a low, spreading, semi-evergreen perennial. The dark green leaves are heart-shaped to round, and the sweetly scented,

V. x wittrockiana

V. odorata

early spring flowers are white, purple or blue. Cultivars are available. (Zones 4–8)

V. tricolor (Johnny-jump-up) is a popular annual. The flowers are purple, white and yellow, usually in combination, though several varieties have flowers in a single colour, often purple.

V. x wittrockiana (pansy) is an annual species that comes in blue, purple, red, orange, yellow, pink or white, often multi-coloured or with face-like markings. Many cultivars are available.

Problems and Pests

Spider mites can be a problem if plants are water stressed.

Historically, violets were raised for scent and, along with rose petals, were used as room deodorizers, usually by strewing the blossoms onto the floor.

Rose

Rosa

Features: dense, arching shrub; fragrant, edible, early summer to fall flowers; orange-red, edible hips **Height:** 90 cm–1.5 m **Spread:** 90 cm–1.8 m

Roses have an incredibly rich history in the culinary arts, crafting, medicine, perfume industry and folklore. Both the petals and the hips are edible. The petals can be highly fragrant and have a pleasing flavour in salads or as a dessert garnish. The hips are not only filled with flavour but also bursting with vitamins, particularly vitamin C.

Starting

Purchase roses as bare-root stock or in containers. Container-grown roses can be

R. gallica var. *officinalis*

planted any time during the growing season. Plant bare-root roses in spring.

Growing

Roses grow best in **full sun** or **partial shade**. The soil should preferably be **average to fertile, humus rich, slightly acidic, moist** and **well drained**, but roses adapt to most soils from silty clay to sand.

Prune roses in summer after they flower. Remove a few of the oldest canes every few years to keep the plants blooming vigorously.

R. gallica var. *officinalis*

Harvesting

The petals can be picked throughout the blooming cycle and used fresh.

Pick rosehips in late summer when they are firm, full and well-coloured. Avoid soft, over-ripe ones. Hips can be used fresh or dried.

Tips

Roses make good additions to mixed borders and beds and can also be used as hedges or as specimens. They are often used on steep banks to prevent soil erosion, and the prickly branches keep people from walking through flower beds and compacting the soil.

Roses can be grown in containers, provided you have a large enough container and are prepared to overwinter them.

Recommended

R. gallica var. *officinalis* (apothecary's rose) is one of the best roses for culinary purposes. It grows 90 cm–1.2 m tall and wide and bears fragrant, semi-double, pink flowers in spring or early summer, followed by orange-red hips. (Zones 3–8)

R. rugosa 'Hansa' is a bushy shrub with arching canes and leathery, deeply veined, bright green leaves. The double flowers are produced all summer. The bright orange hips persist into winter. Other rugosa roses include **'Blanc Double de Coubert,'** with white, double flowers that are produced all summer. (Zones 2–8)

Problems and Pests

Blackspot, rust, mildew, aphids, Japanese beetles, spider mites and slugs can attack roses.

For a rosehip tea rich in vitamin C, trim both blossom and stem ends, halve the hip and scrape out the seeds. Dry the halves on screens indoors until they're as hard as a coffee bean. Use a blender or old coffee mill to grind them up. Rosehips also make a beautiful pink-hued jelly.

R. rugosa

Appendix: Companion Plants

The following plants, arranged in alphabetical order by common name, all provide certain benefits to other plants when growing in proximity to each other, and/or to the garden in general.

Alliums (*Allium* spp.): group includes onions, garlic, leeks, shallots, chives and others; repel and distract slugs, aphids, carrot flies and cabbage worms

Asters (*Aster* spp.): general insect repellents

Borage (*Borago officinalis*): deters tomato worms; companion to tomatoes, squash and strawberries, improving growth and flavour

Calendula (*Calendula officinalis*): repels and distracts nematodes, beet leaf hoppers and other pests

Caraway (*Carum carvi*): loosens soil where it grows; attracts parasitic wasps and parasitic bees

Carrot (*Daucus carota*): attracts assassin bugs, lacewings, parasitic wasps, yellow jackets and other predatory wasps

Chamomile (*Chamaemelum nobile*): encourages other plants such as herbs, including lavender and rosemary, to increase their essential oil content

Chrysanthemums (*Chrysanthemum* spp.): reduce the number of nematodes

Cilantro/Coriander (*Coriandrum sativum*): scent repels aphids, attracts tachinid flies

Dill (*Anethum graveolens*): attracts hoverflies, wasps, tomato horn worms, honeybees, ichneumonid wasps, aphids, spider mites, squash bugs and cabbage looper

Fennel (*Foeniculum vulgare*): attracts ladybugs, syrphid flies and tachinid flies; repels and distracts aphids

Flax (*Linum usitatissimum*): deters potato bugs; companion to carrots and potatoes, improving growth and flavour

Geraniums (*Pelargonium* spp.): can be attractive to caterpillars, luring them away from adjacent plants

Horseradish (*Armoracia rusticana*): planted at corners of potato patch, will discourage potato bugs

Hyssop (*Hyssopus officinalis*): attracts honeybees and butterflies; repels and distracts cabbage moth larvae and cabbage butterflies

Larkspur (*Consolida ajacis*): protects vines against vine beetles

Lavenders (*Lavandula* spp.): general insect repellents; attract pollinating insects; provide protection against borers and mosquitoes

Lavender cotton (*Santolina chamaecyparissus*): general insect repellent

Lovage (*Levisticum officinale*): attracts ichneumonid wasps and ground beetles

Marigolds (*Tagetes* spp.): discourage beetles, nematodes and other pests

Mints (*Mentha* spp.): improve the flavour and growth of cabbage and tomatoes; deter white cabbage moths

Nasturtium (*Tropaeolum majus*): attracts predatory insects; repels and distracts cabbage loopers, squash bugs, white flies and cucumber beetles

Oregano (*Origanum vulgare*): repels and distracts aphids

Parsley (*Petroselinum crispum*): scent deters carrot flies

Peppers, hot (*Capsicum* spp.): produce a chemical that prevents root rot

Petunia (*Petunia* x *hybrida*): deters and distracts leafhoppers, Japanese beetles, aphids and asparagus beetles

Rue (*Ruta graveolens*): deters beetles in roses and raspberries; do not plant near cabbages, basil or sage

Sage (*Salvia officinalis*): deters cabbage moths and carrot flies

Tansy (*Tanacetum vulgare*): companion to roses and raspberries; deters flying insects, Japanese beetles, striped cucumber beetles, ants and squash bugs

Tomato (*Solanum lycopersicum*): when planted near asparagus, deters asparagus beetles

White alyssum (*Lobularia maritime*): reseeds frequently; helps to break up the soil, adding to organic content

Yarrow (*Achillea millefolium*): attracts predatory wasps, ladybugs, hoverflies and damselbugs

COMPANION PLANT RELATIONSHIPS

Plant	Compatible Plants	Incompatible Plants
apricots	basil, tansy	
asparagus	basil, parsley, tomatoes	
beans	most herbs and vegetables	beets, cabbage, garlic, kohlrabi, onions
beets	broccoli, cabbage, chard, garlic, kohlrabi, onions	beans
broccoli	beans, beets, celery, chamomile, cucumbers, lettuce, mint, onions, oregano, potatoes, thyme, rosemary	
cabbage	Alliums, aromatic herbs, beets, celery, chamomile, chard, spinach, potatoes	beans, corn, dill, parsnips, strawberries, tomatoes
carrots	Alliums, bell peppers, grapes, lettuce, peas, sage, tomatoes	dill, parsnips
cauliflower	beans, celery	strawberries
celery	beans, broccoli, cabbage, cauliflower, leeks, nasturtiums, onions, spinach, tomatoes	parsnips

Plant	Compatible Plants	Incompatible Plants
chard, Swiss	beets, cabbage, lavender, onions	
corn	beans, cucumbers, melons, peas, potatoes, squash, tomatoes	cabbage
cucumbers	beans, broccoli, corn, lettuce, peas, sunflowers, radishes	aromatic herbs, potatoes
eggplant	beans, potatoes, spinach	
garlic	beets, lettuce, chamomile, parsnips, peaches, strawberries, tomatoes	beans, peas
grapes	basil, beans, carrots, geraniums, hyssop, peas	
kohlrabi	beets, onions	beans, tomatoes
leeks	carrots, celery, onions	
lettuce	broccoli, carrots, cucumbers, garlic, onions, radishes, strawberries	
melons	corn, radishes	
onions	beets, bell peppers, broccoli, cabbage, carrots, celery, chamomile, chard, kohlrabi, leeks, lettuce, tomatoes, strawberries	beans, peas
parsley	asparagus, tomatoes	
parsnips	beans, bell peppers, garlic, peas, potatoes, radishes	cabbage, carrots, celery
peaches	garlic, tansy	
peas	most herbs and vegetables	garlic, onions, potatoes
peppers, bell	carrots, onions, parsnips, tomatoes	
potatoes	beans, broccoli, cabbage, corn, eggplant, horseradish, marigolds, parsnips	cucumbers, peas, squash, sunflowers, tomatoes, turnips
radishes	cucumbers, lettuce, melons, nasturtiums, parsnips, peas	hyssop
spinach	cabbage, celery, eggplant, strawberries	
squash	corn, nasturtiums	potatoes
strawberries	beans, borage, garlic, lettuce, onions, spinach	cabbage, cauliflower
tomatoes	asparagus, carrots, celery, chives, corn, marigolds, nasturtiums, onions, parsley	cabbage, cucumbers, fennel, kohlrabi, potatoes
turnips	peas	potatoes

Glossary

Acid soil: soil with a pH lower than 7.0

Alkaline soil: soil with a pH higher than 7.0

Annual: a plant that germinates, flowers, sets seeds and dies in one growing season

Basal leaves: leaves that form from the crown, at the base of the plant

Blanching: to deprive a plant or part of a plant of light, resulting in a pale colour and usually a milder flavour

Bolting: when a plant produces flowers and seeds prematurely, usually rendering the plant inedible

Bract: a special, modified leaf at the base of a flower or inflorescence; bracts may be small or large, green or coloured

Cross-pollination: the pollination of one plant by a closely related one. Undesirable if the resulting seeds or fruit lack the expected qualities; beneficial if an improved variety results

Crown: the part of the plant at or just below soil level where the shoots join the roots

Cultivar: a cultivated plant variety with one or more distinct differences from the species, e.g., in flower colour or disease resistance

Damping off: fungal disease causing seedlings to rot at soil level

Deadhead: removing spent flowers to maintain a neat appearance and encourage a long blooming season

Diatomaceous earth: an abrasive dust made from the fossilized remains of diatoms, a species of algae; the scratches it makes on insect bodies causes internal fluids to leak out, and the insects die of dehydration

Direct sow: to sow seeds directly into the garden

Dormancy: a period of plant inactivity, usually during winter or unfavourable conditions

Double flower: a flower with an unusually large number of petals

Drought resistant: can withstand drought for a long time

Drought tolerant: can withstand drought conditions, but only for a limited time

Genus: a category of biological classification between the species and family levels; the first word in a scientific name indicates the genus

Half-hardy: a plant capable of surviving the climatic conditions of a given region if protected from heavy frost or cold

Harden off: to gradually acclimatize plants that have been growing in a protected environment to a harsher environment

Hardy: capable of surviving unfavourable conditions, such as cold weather or frost, without protection

Humus: decomposed or decomposing organic material in the soil

Hybrid: a plant resulting from natural or human-induced cross-breeding between varieties, species or genera

Inflorescence: an arrangement of flowers on a single stem

Invasive: able to spread aggressively and outcompete other plants

Loam: a loose soil composed of clay, sand and organic matter, often highly fertile

Microclimate: an area of beneficial or detrimental growing conditions within a larger area

Mulch: a material (e.g., shredded bark, pine cones, leaves, straw) used to surround a plant to protect it from weeds, cold or heat and to promote moisture retention

Neutral soil: soil with a pH of 7.0

Node: the area on a stem from which a leaf or new shoot grows

Perennial: a plant that takes three or more years to complete its life cycle

pH: a measure of acidity or alkalinity; soil pH influences availability of nutrients for plants

Plantlet: a young or small plant

Potager: an ornamental kitchen garden, often laid out symmetrically with raised beds or low hedge-edged beds

Rhizome: a root-like, food-storing stem that grows horizontally at or just below soil level, from which new shoots may emerge

Rosette: a low, flat cluster of leaves arranged like the petals of a rose

Runner: a modified stem that grows on the soil surface; roots and new shoots are produced at nodes along its length

Seedhead: dried, inedible fruit that contains seeds

Self-seeding: reproducing by means of seeds without human assistance, so that new plants continuously replace those that die

Single flower: a flower with a single ring of typically four or five petals

Spathe: a leaf-like bract that encloses a flower cluster or spike

Species: the fundamental unit of biological classification; the entity from which cultivars and varieties are derived

Standard: a tree or shrub pruned to form a rounded head of branches at the top of a clearly visible stem

Subspecies (subsp.): a naturally occurring, often regional, form of a species, isolated from other sub-species but still potentially interfertile with them

Taproot: a root system consisting of one long main root with smaller roots or root hairs branching from it

Tender: incapable of surviving the climatic conditions of a given region and requiring protection from frost or cold

Tuber: the thick section of a rhizome bearing nodes and buds

Understorey plant: a plant that prefers to grow beneath the canopies of trees in a woodland setting

Variegation: foliage that has more than one colour, often patched, striped or bearing leaf margins of a different colour

Variety (var.): a naturally occurring variant of a species

Index

Boldface type refers to primary vegetable accounts.